Free to Dream

THE MAKING OF A POET:
Langston Hughes

Portrait of Langston Hughes by Nickolas Muray, 1923

Free to Dream

THE MAKING OF A POET:

Langston Hughes

BY AUDREY OSOFSKY

LOTHROP, LEE & SHEPARD BOOKS

NEW YORK

PQLS

11.20

Sources for excerpts and photographs are cited on page 100.

Printed in the United States of America

First Edition   1 2 3 4 5 6 7 8 9 10

Library of Congress Cataloging in Publication Data

Osofsky, Audrey. Free to Dream: the making of a poet: Langston Hughes / by Audrey Osofsky.

p.   cm. Includes bibliographical references and index.

Summary: A biography of the Harlem poet whose works gave voice to the joy and pain of the black experience in America.

ISBN 0-688-10605-6. — ISBN 0-688-10606-4 (lib. bdg.) 1. Hughes, Langston, 1902-1967—Biography—Juvenile literature.

2. Afro-American poets—20th century—Biography—Juvenile literature. [1. Hughes, Langston, 1902-1967. 2. Poets, American.

3. Afro-Americans—Biography.] I. Title.

PS3515.U274Z688 1996 818'.5209—dc20 [B] 95-17354 CIP AC

To You
All you who are dreamers, too,
Help me to make
Our world anew.
I reach out my dreams to you.

—Langston Hughes

Hold fast to dreams
For if dreams die
Life is a broken-winged bird
That cannot fly.

—*Langston Hughes, "Dreams"*

Contents

In the Beginning, the Dream

"Tell me another story," little Langston begged his grandmother.

Her rocker creaked back and forth on the front porch. "Long ago . . . ," she began in a faraway voice.

The boy sitting on her lap listened, his eyes quiet. In the dark shadows he saw

> Black slaves
> Working in the hot sun,
>
> . . . .
>
> And black slaves
> Singing sorrow songs on the banks of a mighty river

He saw heroes holding out hands to the slaves: his grandfather helping them to freedom on the Underground Railroad.

He heard the crackle of guns: John Brown's men at Harpers Ferry, fighting to make black slaves free. He saw one fall, his shawl full of bullet holes: like the shawl his grandmother was wearing.

Langston Hughes listened until the sound of her voice faded away in the summer night. He didn't understand everything his grandmother told him. He was only seven. But he knew the heroes in her stories never cried or felt sorry for themselves. They worked and fought for freedom and never gave up.

He knew about heroes and their dreams.

> Aunt Sue has a head full of stories.
> Aunt Sue has a whole heart full of stories.
>
> . . . .
>
> And the dark-faced child, listening,
> Knows that Aunt Sue's stories are real stories.
> He knows that Aunt Sue never got her stories
> Out of any book at all,
> But that they came
> Right out of her own life.

Langston and Carrie Hughes, 1902

Passed-Around Child

heart full of hurt was the story Langston Hughes told of his childhood. He remembered growing up with a "left-lonesome feeling," wishing that he belonged to a family.

Soon after Langston was born on February 1, 1902, his father left him and his mother and went far away from Joplin, Missouri, to start a new life in Mexico. When Langston was five, his mother, Carrie, packed up her hopes, and with her son and his grandmother, joined James Hughes in Mexico City to try to be a family again.

Their reunion didn't last long. In the middle of the night, Langston woke to a nightmare. His bed was shaking, tarantulas were scurrying out of the walls, his mother was screaming—an earthquake! His father grabbed him and carried him out of the hotel into the safety of the street. Langston clung to him tight. People were praying on their knees, wailing as buildings crumbled around them and the opera house sank into the ground.

The next day, his mother fled with Langston and his grandmother back to the United States, her fear of this foreign land stronger than her feelings for her husband.

Twelve years went by before Langston saw his father again. Growing up, his only memory of his father was of Hughes's strong arms around him, carrying him to safety.

His mother left him lonesome, too, drifting in and out of his life like the sun on a cloudy day. Always on the move looking for a better job, Carrie Hughes left her son with his seventy-three-year-old grandmother, Mary Langston, in Lawrence, Kansas, and tried her luck in other cities. Sometimes his mother would come back to him. "But not often," Langston remembered.

Life was a bitter disappointment to Carrie Hughes. She envisioned herself as an actress on the stage, not as a single parent burdened with a little boy. When she was eighteen, Carrie had recited her poems and read papers at the Inter-State Literary Society founded by her father in Kansas. As she grew older, Carrie loved to dress up in costumes and give dramatic readings.

Once, Langston and another boy were part of her act. Draped in a sheet like a toga, Carrie clasped them close as she recited "The Mother of the Gracchi." Ardently, she enacted the pitiful plight of a Roman mother famous for her love for her sons—her precious "jewels" soon to be torn from her arms.

Langston didn't like the poem and he didn't like wearing a sheet, so he made funny faces to liven up the performance. He rolled his eyes and the audience laughed. He grimaced, mimicking her despair, and they laughed louder. Thinking she had failed to move them with her sad story, Carrie hugged the boys tighter and poured on the theatrics. They laughed even harder. Later, when she found out the part Langston had played, she was not amused. Her son got the worst whipping of his life for ruining his mother's big scene.

Not only had Carrie's father, Charles Langston, encouraged her dramatic and literary interests, but he had also encouraged her education. One of the first blacks to attend Oberlin College, he became associate editor of the black newspaper, the *Historic Times*, and in its pages urged all young people to get a college education.

After her father's death in 1892, Carrie Langston graduated from high school and worked as a clerk in the Lawrence courthouse to help pay for college. Two years later, she completed a ten-week course in primary school teaching and enrolled in the University of Kansas. She took one course in German in the fall and one in English in the spring, then quit to teach in Oklahoma.

It wasn't long before she caught the eye of James Hughes, a former teacher with bigger ambitions, and soon they were married. But they weren't happy together. After Langston was born, the couple separated, and Carrie Hughes was left with a child to support.

She struggled to make a living, for few good jobs were open to a black woman. And because she had married, she couldn't teach, according to the custom of the times. Frustrated with her life, Carrie flitted from city to city seeking greener pastures, while back in Lawrence her son waited, longing to be with his mother.

When Langston was six, his wish came true. Carrie returned and took him with her to Topeka, Kansas, where she worked as a stenographer for a lawyer. Home was a room over a plumbing store downtown, with a one-pot "monkey-stove" to cook on and keep them warm. Langston's job was to search the alleys after the stores closed, looking for old wooden boxes to burn in their stove. He stomped on the boxes to break them up, and Carrie chopped them with a hatchet for kindling.

Together they explored a magical place covered with green vines. A library, his mother told him. The hushed room, shiny tables, and helpful librarians delighted Langston, and he fell in love with the beautiful world of books, so different from the life he knew.

Sometimes, as a special treat, Langston and his mother took the train to Kansas City to visit Uncle Desalines and his barbershop. The clackety-clack of the train wheels and the clanging bells set Langston's imagination spinning.

What new places would he see? What new people would he meet? He loved the excitement of going on a trip, the tingling feeling that promised surprises.

Best of all, his mother took him to the theater as often as she could afford it. When the bright lights of the stage brought *Buster Brown, Uncle Tom's Cabin,* and *Little Lord Fauntleroy* to life, Langston discovered another magic world of make-believe.

But the real world was colored white. Langston found that out on the first day of school. When he tried to enroll at Harrison Street School near his home, the principal

The Home of Langston and Carrie Hughes in Topeka, Kansas

turned the first grader away. You don't belong here, Langston was told. You have to go to the black school.

Carrie Hughes was angry. Washington School was across the railroad tracks, on the other side of town. She protested that her son was too young to walk that far through the city streets alone. The principal insisted it was school policy.

Undaunted, Carrie appealed to the school board and pleaded her case. Her dramatic flair came in handy for Langston that day. In a decision that was rare for the times, Carrie won her appeal, and her black child was enrolled in the white school.

Her son, however, had to fight a battle every day. His teacher wanted Langston to learn a lesson: that he didn't belong in a white classroom. She made him sit at the end of the last row, and she didn't let a day go by without making hurtful comments about him. Langston kept his feelings locked up tight. His smile never showed how sad he felt inside.

One day, his teacher took licorice sticks away from a boy. "You don't want to eat these," she said loudly for the class to hear. "They'll make you black like Langston. You don't want to be black, do you?" Everyone turned and stared at Langston.

After school, kids sometimes called him names and chased him, throwing tin cans and stones. Langston ran for home, wondering why the kids didn't like him. One boy always came to his rescue and yelled at their classmates to stop. Then a few other boys also stood up for him.

"So I learned early not to hate *all* white people," he would write. He believed that the race problem wasn't caused by skin color, but by people "who have small minds, or small spirits."

No matter how he was treated, Langston loved to learn. Every morning he went to school with a smile, his clothes clean and neatly pressed, his eyes bright. Even his teacher, who never stopped picking on him, grudgingly marked him an excellent student.

Before the school year

The Harrison Street School in Topeka, Kansas

ended, his mother took him out of first grade, and Langston's happy days with her were over. Carrie Hughes again left her son with his grandmother in Lawrence, while she moved to Colorado to find another job.

"I was unhappy for a long time, and very lonesome, living with my grandmother," Langston remembered. He wished he had a brother or sister to play with. It was too quiet in the house with only his grandmother around.

Mary Langston was a proud woman, strict and set in her ways. She was proud that she had been one of the first black women to attend Oberlin College. And proud that she had never been a slave. She was born free, in North Carolina, because she was part Cherokee. Her grandson thought she looked like an Indian, with her copper-colored skin and straight, glossy black hair almost to her waist.

Her first husband, Lewis Sheridan Leary, had died a hero at Harpers Ferry, and Mary wore his bullet-riddled shawl with pride. Summer nights on the front porch, she told his story to Langston: how he had fought by the side of John Brown to make black slaves free. And when her grandson went to bed, she would cover him with the freedom shawl.

Charles Langston, her second husband, fought for freedom, too. In 1858, he helped rescue a runaway slave on the Underground Railroad and was charged with the crime of breaking the Fugitive Slave Law. In a fiery speech in the courtroom, he denounced racial prejudice as the crime. The judge was so impressed that he gave the abolitionist the minimum sentence of twenty days in jail and a hundred-dollar fine. But the judge couldn't silence Charles Langston's speeches. As an editor and politician, he continued to speak out against discrimination.

But Mary's pride in her husband's great speeches couldn't pay the mortgage man when Charles Langston died. Poor as she was, Mary Langston was too proud to take in laundry or work as a maid, as many black women did. She rented rooms to college students instead. Sometimes she rented her whole house for ten dollars a month while she and Langston moved in with her friends, the Reeds.

But they lived with worry as a constant roomer. Afraid the mortgage man would take their house away, they scrimped to pay the interest. Often they didn't have enough to eat, and Langston had to wear made-over clothes, even ladies' shoes given to his grandmother. Kids made fun of him and called him a sissy.

In the fall of 1909, Langston went to Pinckney School, where all black children in the

Langston Hughes's Grandmother, Mary Langston, 1910

first three grades were taught in one room. As a second grader, he was lucky to have a good teacher. Mary J. Dillard, who had admired his grandfather Charles as a "deep thinker," remembered Langston as "a dreamy little boy."

The next summer, when Langston was eight, his mother was working in Kansas City. A friend of Carrie's sent her son to Lawrence to visit for a few weeks. Happy to have someone to play with, Langston showed his new friend how to make marbles out of black mud, rolling them round in the palms of his hands and drying them in the sun. Sometimes the boys didn't wait for the mud to dry. They threw the marbles at the back of the woodshed and laughed when they went *splat* and stuck. Sometimes they threw the mud balls at each other and laughed even harder. At night, the boys ran around the yard catching fireflies. They peeked into their cupped hands, watching the lightning bugs' amber glow, then set them free.

His Kansas City friend stayed only a few days. He wrote to his mother that he wanted to go home because they had nothing to eat but salt pork and wild dandelions.

Langston was heartbroken. "I cried when he showed me the letter. . . . And I never wanted my mother to invite any more little boys to stay with me at my grandmother's house."

When school started, Langston was eager to play with his classmates. His grandmother, however, gave him strict orders to come straight home from school. She always had chores for him to do. After he pumped water, carried in wood, and ran errands, he wanted to play with the neighborhood boys in the vacant lot. But his grandmother's pride kept him lonely. Worried that the white boys would pick on her grandson, she made him stay by her side. Mary Langston never forgot how her pride had been hurt when a white church refused to let her join.

Sitting near her rocker, reading, Langston listened to the boys playing ball and yelling, "Catch it! Catch it!" He ached inside, hearing the boys laughing, playing together, while he sat alone.

"She kept him kind of under her thumb," his schoolmate John Taylor recalled.

One year stretched to another, yet Langston still stayed with his grandmother. On rare occasions, to Langston's great joy, he and his mother met at the train station in Kansas City and went to the music hall together. After the footlights dimmed, the bright glimpse of his heart's desire faded away as his mother waved good-bye. For six lonely years, except for two summers together, Langston waited for his mother to claim him, like a piece of baggage she had left behind and forgotten.

When he was thirteen, his grandmother died, and Langston was left all alone. He didn't cry; the heroes in her stories never cried. He knew it wouldn't help. And it wouldn't stop the mortgage man from getting the house in the end.

Langston hoped his mother would come and care for him now. But like an orphan, he was taken in by friends of his grandmother's. Longing to be part of a family, he called them Auntie and Uncle Reed.

Hurt by his mother's rejection, wondering why she didn't want him with her, Langston turned deeper into himself: "I believed in books more than in people." In books, people never let him down, and dreams always came true.

> "I were a passed-around child. While my mother was not there and my father was not there and they was separated, I were left with whoever would take care of me when they was not there.
>
> "Nobody was mean to me, and I do not know why I had that left-out feeling, but I did, I guess because nobody ever said, 'You're mine,' and I did not really belong to nobody."

Langston Hughes and James Reed, 1914

A Bright Bowl of Brass

Langston at last had plenty to eat at the Reeds'. They had a garden and chickens and cows, and they owned their little house near the railroad tracks. No mortgage man could ever take it away.

He helped out by herding cows to pasture, chopping wood, and collecting eggs from the hens. And he ate and ate—hoecake and molasses, salt pork and greens, peas and onions dewy fresh from the garden, cold, creamy milk— and topped it off with Auntie Reed's apple dumplings and butter sauce.

"For me, there have never been any better people in the world," Langston would write. "I loved them very much."

Auntie Reed made him go to Sunday school and church, and though Langston complained a little, he was fascinated by the vibrant rhythms of gospel singing and the dramatic sermons. She called Uncle Reed a sinner for staying home every Sunday and washing his overalls "in a big iron pot in the back yard." But both the Reeds were good people, Langston believed, "the one who went to church and the one who didn't."

To earn pocket money, Langston gathered maple seeds in the spring and sold them to the seed store. He delivered newspapers and the *Saturday Evening Post* magazine. In seventh grade, he got his first real job, working in an old hotel. He cleaned toilets, swept the lobby, and scoured and shined brass spittoons for fifty cents a week.

The only chore he disliked was emptying the slimy spittoons in the alley, rinsing them out, and scrubbing them clean. Yet after they were polished, Langston felt proud when he looked around the dingy lobby. The six brass bowls gleamed like gold. They'd be covered with tobacco juice and spit again tomorrow, but he'd clean them bright, he'd make them shine.

Now that he had his own money to spend, Langston enjoyed riding the streetcar that circled the town for a nickel. He thought it would be fun to be a streetcar conductor when he grew up. He'd let all the kids ride free to Woodland Park for the Children's Day Party. The black kids, too.

He remembered how excited he was when he was eight and the *Daily Journal* had advertised: FREE PICNIC AND ENTERTAINMENT FOR ALL CHILDREN! He couldn't wait to ride on the merry-go-round, swing up high in the Ferris wheel, shoot-the-shoots, and go in the crazy house.

And he remembered how disappointed he was when the paper announced two days before the party, on August 17, 1910:

> The Journal knows the colored children have no desire to attend a social event
> of this kind and that they will not want to go. This is purely a social affair and of
> course everyone in town knows what that means.

Langston knew what rejection meant; he was no stranger to the feeling. To escape a world where he was not wanted, he entered his fantasy world, where anything was possible. At the movies, he could laugh at Charlie Chaplin, or be scared for poor Pearl White in *The Clutching Claw,* and forget his troubles.

Then one day his fun ended. The owner of the Patee Theater shoved back his nickel and snapped, "Your people can't come anymore." She pointed to a new sign: NO COLORED ADMITTED. His hopes crushed, Langston could only listen to the white kids as they talked and laughed about movies they had seen.

Lawrence Daily Journal

JOURNAL'S ASSOCIATED PRESS BEATS OTHER PAPERS HERE 4 HOURS

ALL THE NEWS TO EVERY-ONE—THE JOURNAL

LAWRENCE, KANSAS, WEDNESDAY EVENING, AUGUST 17, 1910.

NO. 196.

Lawrence Daily Journal, August 17, 1910

ABOUT THAT PARTY

On Friday the Journal Will Entertain the Little Folks

The Journal's party will be given on Friday from 3 o'clock to 6:30 in Woodland Park.

The Journal hopes that all the children between the ages of 6 and 13 will attend its party. It is expecting a great time. Special street cars, accompanied by ladies to look after the children will be in waiting at the Journal office and take the children out to the park. Upon arriving there the fine vaudeville and picture show will give a special performance for guests of the Journal. After that the children will play around and be entertained by the band. Cars will be in waiting to bring the children home. On the return trip each child desiring a transfer will be supplied so that all of the children can be taken to their homes. The Journal has been asked if the colored children will be in attendance. The Journal knows the colored children have no desire to attend a social event of this kind and that they will not want to go. This is purely a social affair and of course everyone in town knows what that means.

The Journal is anxious for the children with it and have a good time. The Journal has never given a party before and this one to be a great success. Journal office at 3 Friday.

When road shows came to town, Langston tried the Bowersock Opera House. The ticket lady took his quarter, but told him to sit at the back of the balcony, in "Nigger Heaven." It felt like heaven to Langston, "thrilled at the world across the footlights."

Beneath Langston's quiet exterior, however, he was Mary Langston's grandson. Proud of his heritage, he rebelled when his seventh-grade teacher moved all the black students to a separate row. Segregation's ugly Jim Crow laws, setting his people apart and denying them rights, made him angry. Quickly, he made signs saying JIM CROW ROW, put them on the desks, and ran out into the playground yelling, "Teacher's got a Jim Crow row!"

When the principal tried to calm him down, Langston punched him and he was expelled. The next day, four black mothers and a doctor marched to school in protest. The segregated seating was changed, and Langston was allowed back in the classroom. "He wouldn't budge an inch until he got what he wanted," John Taylor recalled admiringly.

His classmates were surprised at his passion, for they all knew Langston as quiet, well-mannered, and friendly. "He always carried a smile," remembered Taylor. "Just everybody loved him."

At recess, instead of playing games with the class, Langston often stayed by himself, writing on scraps of paper. Sometimes his friends would ask him what he was writing. Shyly, he'd show them. "We didn't think too much about it," admitted Luella Patterson, "but we'd say, 'Oh, Langston's writin' another poem.'"

"Poetry was his hobby," John Taylor noted. "Instead of gettin' out and playing football, baseball, and all the other kinds of balls the rest of us played, he chose to isolate himself and work on his poems. . . . And he would read 'em to the English class."

His English teacher didn't recall any poetry. "He was a bad combination—part Indian, part Nigra, and part white. . . . I don't remember that Langston had any talent."

His schoolmates remembered Langston differently, as an "A student" and "tops in the class."

In school sports, he didn't have a chance to excel. An invisible sign—NO COLORED ADMITTED—blocked his way. Although he could run fast and clear the high jump over his head, only white boys could enter track meets. Langston could only watch. He couldn't join the swim team, either. The school used the YMCA pool and showers, and black children were not allowed in the YMCA.

But Langston knew his mind was free. No one could put up a sign saying NO IMAGINATION ALLOWED. He heard the blues played by a blind guitar player on a Kansas City street corner and kept on dreaming.

Clean the spittoons, boy!

. . . .

The steam in hotel kitchens,
And the smoke in hotel lobbies,
And the slime in hotel spittoons:
Part of my life.
    Hey, boy!

. . . .

A bright bowl of brass is beautiful to the Lord.

. . . .

A clean bright spittoon all newly polished—
At least I can offer that.
    Com'mere, boy!

Langston with Carrie Hughes, Homer and Young Kit Clark, and Unidentified Friend c. 1916

Handful of Dream Dust

Langston was almost
fourteen years old before his mother finally claimed him.
She had remarried and was living in Lincoln, Illinois, with
her husband and his two-year-old son, Kit. When Langston
found out he had a "brother," too, he was happy. A real
family at last!

He liked his stepfather, Homer Clark, and called him
Dad. Homer was easygoing and kind, "a good sport." But
like Carrie, he was a wanderer, always looking for a better
job in another city. On the day of Langston's eighth-grade
graduation in May 1916, Homer Clark left town again, and
left behind a disappointed boy. Langston had wanted his
dad to see him graduate and hear him read his class poem.

He had been elected class poet, Langston believed,
because his teacher, Ethel Welch, had said a poem needed
rhythm, and "most white people think . . . that *all* Negroes
can sing and dance, and have a sense of rhythm." He wrote
sixteen verses praising every teacher and the class, and after
he read it, everyone clapped.

"That was the way I began to write poetry," Langston

wrote years later in his autobiography, *The Big Sea.* He never mentioned the earlier poems his Kansas school friends recalled. Perhaps his first efforts didn't seem like real poems to him.

Soon after graduation, Langston had to leave his friends and move again. Homer Clark had found a job as machinist in a steel mill in Cleveland, Ohio. Because World War I was raging in Europe, steel mills needed workers, no matter what their color. Before the war, only menial jobs—or none at all—were open to blacks. Now Homer Clark could earn a good living.

Color did matter when the family looked for a place to live. In the days of the Great Migration, when blacks by the thousands were streaming into the North, looking for work and a better way of life, housing was hard to find. Many lived in sheds and garages, and if they were fortunate enough to find attic or basement rooms, their rent was doubled or tripled. After a long search, the family found a basement apartment and settled in.

Luckily for Langston, Cleveland's Central High School was color-blind. Most of its

Track and Field, 1920

students were children of European immigrants, a vital mixture of Russians, Poles, Hungarians, and Italians. Because everyone was a member of a minority, Langston fit right in. His smile was a magnet that drew many friends to him. They called him Lang and elected him to the student council.

No longer was he standing on the outside looking in. He joined the school track team: ran the quarter mile, won awards for the high jump, and ran relays on the city championship team.

His sophomore English teacher, Ethel Weimer, encouraged him to write and introduced him to the poetry of Walt Whitman and Carl Sandburg. Langston called Sandburg his "guiding star" and was inspired to write a poem about the steel mills when he was fifteen. He had seen how the heat of the furnaces had worn out his stepfather:

The mills
That grind and grind,
That grind out steel
And grind away the lives
Of men—

. . . .

The mills—
Grinding new steel,
Old men.

Some of Langston's poetry was published in the Central High *Monthly*, but he kept most of his poems to himself. He felt that they were "very much a part of me. And I was afraid other people might not like them or understand them." When poems came to

Cleveland Central High School

him, "from somewhere inside," he jotted them down on anything handy and copied them later into a notebook, "for poems are like rainbows: they escape you quickly."

Happy at school, nourished by its warm support, Langston thrived like a garden in spring. But at home, the old pattern repeated. His mother and stepfather separated, and soon after, Carrie left for Chicago with Kit, hoping to find Homer and reconciliation.

Left alone, Langston moved to a rooming house to finish his sophomore year. To fill his lonely hours, he taught drawing and painting to neighborhood children at the community center, the Playground House. In a cozy book-filled room, he stayed late into the night, reading.

When the school year ended, he joined his mother and Kit in Chicago, where she was working as a maid. She had found Homer, but his "travelin' blues" had come on again and he was gone. Langston got a job as delivery boy for a ladies' hat shop and tried to save money to return to Cleveland for his junior year. All summer, he sweltered in their one small room next to the elevated train tracks. He slept fitfully. Every time a train rumbled by, he woke with a start and shook "as though a sudden dragon were rushing at the bed."

The steamy summer finally came to an end. And so would his plans for the future, if Langston's mother had her way. She demanded that he quit school and get a job to help her. Langston felt sick inside. He knew other children who were forced to quit school at sixteen and go to work. It didn't make any sense to him. "What kind of job can I get that would pay enough to make it worthwhile leaving school?" he argued. He was determined not to give in.

Langston left his mother and returned to high school in Cleveland. With the little money he had saved, he rented an attic room and cooked his meals in the kitchen of the rooming house. Sometimes his best friend, Sartur Andrzejewski, invited him to a Polish dinner of sweet-and-sour cabbage. Most of the time, Langston ate rice. It was the only thing he knew how to cook. He boiled it to a gummy paste and ate rice and hot dogs, hot dogs and rice, every night.

Lonely, he'd read himself to sleep, and dream.

> *Gather out of star-dust*
> *Earth-dust,*
> *Cloud-dust,*
> *Storm-dust,*
> *And splinters of hail,*
> *One handful of dream-dust*
> *Not for sale.*

Langston and Carrie Hughes, c. 1916

Deep like the Rivers

In Langston's junior year, the world was his classroom, and he was exposed to ideas that shaped his life. On November 11, 1918, he ran out into the streets to celebrate the armistice, the end of World War I. But the war fought to save democracy did not save jobs for blacks when white soldiers returned. And black soldiers could not find jobs. The grandson of Charles Langston would make freedom from discrimination a major theme in his speeches and writings.

Ten Days That Shook the World, John Reed's book about the Russian Revolution, "shook Central High School, too," Langston would write. The students were excited about the Bolsheviks' promises of "all land to the peasants, all factories to the workers" and an end of racial and religious persecution. To Langston and the children of Eastern European immigrants, it sounded like utopia.

His interest in socialism had been sparked by his Jewish friends, who had taken him to lectures by the Socialist leader Eugene Debs and lent him books and the *Liberator* magazine. Seeds were planted in an idealistic poet, and in years to come, Langston would write poems of social protest.

Langston with Friends, 1919

He loved school, the teachers, the stimulating student body, and the many extracurricular activities that filled his days: secretary of the French Club, member of the student council and track team, and editor in chief of the "Belfry Owl." Yet he still found time to write poetry, and began to write short stories. They, too, were published in the Central High *Monthly.*

In the spring of his seventeenth year, his mother and Kit returned to Cleveland, and Langston joined them in a small basement apartment. He was happy to be part of a family again.

Suddenly, after twelve silent years, a message came from his father. James Hughes wrote Langston that he would be passing through town on business: "You are to accompany me to Mexico for the summer."

His mother was furious. "It is just like your devilish, evil father! When you get big enough to work and help me earn a living, he wants to come and take you off to Mexico!"

Langston didn't want to hurt her feelings, but he was eager to see his father. In his mind, he pictured James Hughes as a "strong, bronze cowboy, in a big Mexican hat."

"After all I have done for you!" his mother cried.

Homer Clark, back from his wanderings, encouraged his stepson to go. Hoping that Homer would calm his mother down, Langston counted the days until June. Then he packed his suitcase with his track letter at the top, his award for the high jump and the 440-yard relays. He couldn't wait to show it to his father.

When he finally met James Hughes, Langston tried to hide his disappointment. His father didn't look like a cowboy at all. He was a small man with a bushy mustache, who walked and talked fast, and Langston could tell he was used to ordering people around.

"He never said a word about being glad to see me," Langston would write. They boarded the train to Toluca, Mexico—and the most miserable summer of Langston's life.

A bitter man, James Hughes had left the United States believing that blacks had no chance to better themselves. After studying law for years, he had not been allowed to take the bar exam to be a lawyer because of his color. Angry and frustrated, he fled to Mexico, where he could use his knowledge of law. In time, James Hughes had become wealthy and owned a big ranch in the mountains.

James Hughes, 1930

But he didn't help his struggling family. He hoarded his money as if he could never pile up enough to cover the bitterness in his heart. Consumed with contempt for all poor people, blacks as well as Mexicans, James Hughes called them ignorant and lazy, and "thought it was their own fault that they were poor."

"I like Negroes," Langston protested. "We have plenty of fun." They tried to enjoy life, he believed, even if they were poor. He thought of his mother, going to shows and dances, and his stepfather, getting together with friends to play cards and have a good time. All his father cared about was making money—to save. Never to spend, never to enjoy.

He wouldn't take his son to see a bullfight or the floating gardens of Lake Xochimilco. Langston wanted to climb to the top of the Nevado de Toluca, the snowcapped volcano he saw in the distance every day. He wondered if the lakes in its crater looked as magical as they sounded in Spanish: Laguna del Sol and Laguna de la Luna, the Lakes of the Sun and the Moon.

James Hughes thought sight-seeing was a waste of time. Instead, he forced his son to study typing and bookkeeping, which Langston didn't like and wasn't very good at. "Seventeen and you can't add yet!" his father would shout. "Hurry up! Hurry up!" And his son would make more mistakes.

The summer dragged on, and Langston's depression grew deeper. He ended up in a hospital, dizzy and feverish, his stomach turning over and over, his hatred for his father erupting inside in "anger like a tidal wave."

When September came at last, he headed home, glad to leave his father far behind. Crossing the border, Langston knew he was in the United States when a soda fountain clerk refused to serve him because he was black. And the news that greeted him was grim. In the "Red Summer of 1919," race riots had swept the country; hundreds of blacks had died in labor protests; and in Chicago, thirty-eight had died when a black swimmer crossed an invisible line in the water separating a "white" beach from a "black" beach. By the end of the year, riots would inflame more than twenty cities and seventy-six blacks would be lynched.

How could his father be so heartless as to hate his own people? Langston grieved. Nurtured by his grandmother's hero-stories, he rebelled against James Hughes's prejudice; his father's contempt for blacks strengthened Langston's pride in his race.

As a senior, Langston proudly wore his school sweater, decorated with club pins and track-and-field letters. He was elected to the student council again and was editor in chief of the *Annual*. "Langston Hughes is crazy about 'eats,'" the yearbook commented, and his "soulful eyes" made the list of ideal features of Central High students.

His warm smile and easy laugh won him many friends, and they went as a group to plays and to lectures. Although he took a girl to a symphony concert, Langston didn't have much

Langston Hughes
5709 Longfellow Ave.
Scientific Course
"Lang"
Editor of Annual
Student Council
Track '18 '19 '20
Treas. Home Garden
Club '18
Pres. A. C. A. '19
Sec. French Club '19
Class Poet

Cleveland Central High School Yearbook Portrait, 1920

interest in dating. Busy writing, studying, acting in a play, and working in a hotel after school, he spent most of his free time with his Polish friend Sartur, whose "main ambition was to remain a bachelor."

When spring came, Langston liked to go to dances at other schools. In the gym of Longwood High, he fell in love with a girl in a red dress, her "skin like rich chocolate," and was inspired to write his first poem in praise of his people:

> *When Susanna Jones wears red*
> *Her face is like an ancient cameo*
> *Turned brown by the ages.*
>
> *Come with a blast of trumpets,*
> *Jesus!*
>
> *When Susanna Jones wears red*
> *A queen from some time-dead Egyptian night*
> *Walks once again.*

He had found his voice and the subject of his true love—the black race.

Langston was elected class poet again, but this time he had a notebook full of poems, and another notebook filled with verses. Graduating with honors in June 1920, he hoped to go to college, somehow.

His mother had her own plans. She wanted him to go to work and be "of some use to her."

Langston's stomach churned. It was the same old argument. "I could be of more help to you once I get an education," he insisted. He knew that he could get only low-paying jobs right out of high school. If he worked as a porter or busboy, what kind of life would they have? He'd be stuck in a dead-end job forever.

His mother never let up. "How would you look going off to college and me working like a dog!" she complained.

When his father wrote, summoning him to Mexico to discuss his future, Langston tried to block out his deep anger. His only hope was his father. Bracing himself for his mother's irate scenes, he packed his bags for Toluca. His mother was so upset, she didn't even say good-bye.

With a heavy heart, Langston left for Mexico. "I felt pretty bad when I got on the train," he remembered. "My best poems were all written when I felt the worst."

At sunset, as the train crossed a bridge, he sat looking out the window at the Mississippi River. On the back of an envelope, he quickly jotted down words to a poem—the mighty, muddy river calling up the deep past, setting him to dreaming:

> *I've known rivers:*
> *I've known rivers ancient as the world and older than the*
> > *flow of human blood in human veins.*
> *My soul has grown deep like the rivers.*

Support Your Team

THE BELFRY OWL

Vote For Bond Issue

VOL. I. NO. 1.   CENTRAL HIGH SCHOOL, CLEVELAND, O., THURSDAY, OCTOBER 28, 1920.   FIVE CENTS.

Central High to Celebrate Diamond Jubilee

GARDEN CLUB
HOLDS FLOWER SALE

Annual Event Is Picturesque Scene

Proceeds to Beautify Garden

A riot of color and the clean, woodsy fragrance of thousands of chrysanthemums greeted the teachers and students of Central as they entered the hall Tuesday morning. The occasion was the annual flower sale of the Home Garden Club.

Most of the flowers were donations of friends of Central, but some of them came from the city gardens.

The club sold more chrysanthemums in a day other than any cosmos, dahlias, marigolds and pansies were also in demand.

The teachers responded readily, showing their love for blooms by displaying them on their desks. Flowers seemed to be growing everywhere, even in the boys' buttonholes, and in the hair of the girls.

The Japanese effect gained by lanterns and screens decorated by art students, was a pleasing feature.

The proceeds of the sale are to be used by the Garden Club to beautify further the school grounds. Central is indebted to this club for the formal garden and the pergola. Miss Helen M. Chesnutt is faculty advisor.

A Tragedy Averted

There is great rejoicing in the heart of Mr. Jesse Beer, physics teacher at Central, because of the return of a long-lost book which had evidently been taken by mistake, or had just strayed away as physics books sometimes do. The reason for Mr. Beer's distress over the loss was not that he was in need of the marginal notes containing valuable suggestions for the teaching of physics. No, it wasn't that. His concern lay in the possibility of little Johnny Jones's blossoming forth with as much knowledge of the subject as the renowned physicists, Messrs. Marple and Peer themselves.

The Initiation into High-School-Dom

LANGSTON HUGHES, '20
ACCEPTS POSITION
IN MEXICAN SCHOOL

Bullfights Among His Pastimes

Teaching English in a Mexican high school and for recreation attending bullfights, is the unusual experience this year of Langston Hughes, '20.

Students of Central remember Mr. Hughes as editor of the Annual and of the Monthly. He also took an active part in dramatics, playing leading roles in several plays last year. For two years he was Central's high jumper at track meets with a record of five feet six inches.

Mr. Hughes's interest in sports explains his liking for the more violent pastimes of Mexico. An account of his impressions of teaching and of Mexican life in general will appear in a future issue of the Belfry Owl.

CENTRAL'S ENROLLMENT
LARGEST IN HISTORY

"The congestion in Central High School should be relieved. I shall do all in my power to that end," said Principal Edward L. Harris at the first rhetoricals of the term.

Central has now 2,300 pupils, more than ever before, and is a more than the capacity of the building. The class rooms are all crowded. Every nook and corner is occupied.

"But, if we all pull together," said Mr. Harris, "there is nothing we cannot accomplish."

BLOOD TRANSFUSION
NECESSARY T...

Former Cent...

Cent...
a form...
'20, ...
rob...
...some
...gar-
...
...chrysanthe-
...olds and
...and.
...ed readily,
...blooms by
...their desks.
...be growing
...e boys' but-
...hair of the

...gained by
...corated by
...ng feature.
...le are to
...Club to
...grounds.
...lub for
...rgola.
...fac-

Oldest High School
West of Allegheny to Observe Anniversary

PLANS ARE BEING MADE

Established in 1846, Central, the oldest public high school in Ohio, will celebrate her 75th anniversary this coming June. Plans are being made to observe the occasion fittingly.

Like most old institutions, Central boasts of a noble past. The first record book of the school reveals items of compelling interest. John Bradburn, whose portrait hangs in the office, head of school managers, was the first to labor for the establishment of Central. The resolution, that a boys' high school be founded, was adopted. A room was hired in the basement of the Universalist Church, on Prospect street. July, 1846, saw the school opened at... Andrew Freese as... ...Boys.
...ed at-
...pro-

Form...

Centra...
a former...
'20, here...
robbery...
"Petre...
everything...
save him...
charge Sa...
Twice...
given the...
Petre's...
as a quiet...
a ready...

THEO...

Hello, Everybody!   I'm Here to...

The Belfry Owl, October 28, 1920

One-Way Ticket

Lonesome and unhappy, Langston wrote many poems in Toluca that long, hot summer. He was anxious about college starting in the fall and his father's silence on the subject. He spent the summer studying Spanish, reading books, learning to ride bareback on his black horse, Tito, and waiting for his father to talk about his future.

Late in the summer, when Langston had learned to ride fast and shoot straight, his father took him up the mountain trails to visit his ranch. They went with an armed party, for bandits roamed the hills, and James Hughes wasn't taking any chances. He had been robbed twice before on the road to his ranch, left "standing in a pine forest in nothing but his underwear."

The Rancho de Cienguillas spread over the whole side of a mountain, and Langston thought it was "lonesome-looking country." He felt sorry for the peons huddled by fires outside their mud huts, wrapped in blankets to keep out the mountain cold. He shared their supper of tortillas and red beans and slept on the floor of a hut.

In the morning, as they rode to the silver mines near his ranch, James Hughes unveiled his plan. After his son finished his mining-engineering studies in Switzerland and Germany, he would work here at the mines.

Langston almost fell off his horse. "But I can't be a mining engineer!" he protested. "I'm no good at mathematics." And how could he learn physics and chemistry in a foreign language?

"Engineering is something that will make you some money," his father said impatiently. "What do you want to do, live like a nigger all your life? Look at your mother, waiting table in a restaurant! Don't you want to get anywhere?"

In the back of Langston's mind, an idea was growing. Hesitantly he told his father that he wanted to be a writer.

"A writer?" James Hughes sneered. "A writer? Do they make any money?"

Always money. His father's whole life was built on money, Langston thought angrily. And now he was trying to build his son's life on money—just as his mother was. Langston was determined to stand up to his father, too. He would live his own life.

James Hughes was as stubborn as his son. He ordered Langston to stay in Mexico until he "decided to act wisely." They rode down the mountain in silence, Langston seething inside at his father's domineering attitude. James Hughes had reentered his life as a stranger. What right did he have to decide his future?

In the fall, his father still wouldn't yield: Europe or nothing. Langston wouldn't yield, either. He decided to get away on his own. He would teach English in private schools and save his money until he had enough to leave.

He didn't save all his money. On most weekends, he went to the bullfights. When Langston tried to write about them, he couldn't make their drama come alive on paper. He was more successful with his poems, an article about Mexican games, and a one-act play, *The Gold Piece*. He sent them to a black children's magazine in New York, *Brownies' Book*. They were accepted and the editor, Jessie Fauset, wanted more.

Langston sent the poem he had written on the train, "The Negro Speaks of Rivers." It was published in their adult black magazine, the *Crisis,* in June 1921. He was nineteen years old.

"Did they pay you anything?" his father asked.

They hadn't, but Langston didn't care. He was happy to be published, to know that other people thought he was a writer, too.

Maybe his father was impressed, after all. James Hughes finally gave up his demands and offered to pay for any college his son chose. It had taken a year to change his mind.

During that long year, Langston's heart had been leading him to Harlem, the black mecca he had heard and read about, where musicians, writers, and artists were busting out in creative vitality. He wanted to see the new Broadway musical *Shuffle Along* and hear Florence Mills sing. The toe-tapping beat of the Harlem Renaissance called to him, Be part of us!

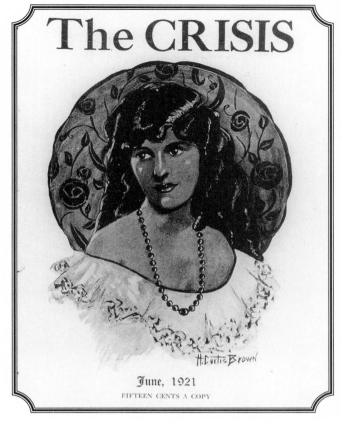

The CRISIS

H. Curtis Brown

June, 1921
FIFTEEN CENTS A COPY

The Crisis, June, 1921

Take Harlem's heartbeat,
Make a drumbeat,
Put it on a record, let it whirl.

Most of all, Langston longed to be with his own people. After years of growing up without a real family, living in a white neighborhood in Lawrence, attending white schools, adapting to Mexican ways, existing alienated from his father and emotionally isolated from his mother, Langston was tired of feeling like an outsider, of not belonging anywhere. He chose Columbia University in New York City, the school on Harlem's doorstep.

Happy to leave Mexico at last, Langston boarded a train for the coast and said good-bye to his father. He would never see him again.

At Veracruz on the Gulf of Mexico, Langston lost his heart. Shining silver to the rim of

One-Way Ticket

the sky (and how far beyond?), the big sea opened its arms to him, promising adventure, as it would all his life. Sharing his cabin with an old Cuban and his crate of chickens, Langston sailed for New York, dreaming of new horizons.

I pick up my life
And take it away
On a one-way ticket—
Gone up North,
Gone out West,
Gone!

Parade on Seventh Avenue in Harlem c. 1920s

Stars over Harlem

hen Langston stepped out of the subway in Harlem and saw hundreds of blacks, he took a deep breath and smiled. He "wanted to shake hands with them, speak to them." For the first time in his life, Langston felt that he belonged. In his heart, Harlem was home:

> *When for years, I had been seeking*
> *Life in places gentler speaking*
> *Until I came to this near street*
> *And found Life—stepping on my feet!*

Columbia, however, made him feel like an unwelcome guest. The housing clerk took one look at Langston and told him all the dorm rooms were taken. The freshman insisted that his father had paid for his room months before. The mix-up was solved when his reservation was found. Since it had been mailed from Mexico, the school had assumed he was Mexican and had assigned him a room. After a flurry of consultations among the officials, Langston was given a room in Hartley Hall.

47

It was a dreary year. Columbia wasn't fun like high school. It was cold and impersonal like a big factory. Few students would have anything to do with him, except Yee Sing Chun, a Chinese classmate. When Langston tried to write for the school paper, the *Spectator,* the editors assigned him to cover fraternity and society news, knowing full well that blacks could never enter a fraternity house or attend a party.

Adding to his troubles, his mother moved to New York. She had separated from Homer Clark again, and Langston had to stretch his allowance to help her until she found a job. To save money, he borrowed textbooks from the library instead of buying them, and washed his socks and handkerchiefs by hand.

Every month he ran out of money, and his father angrily demanded that he account for every penny. "All gone" seemed accurate enough to Langston, but James Hughes insisted on more detail—plus A's in all his courses.

Depressed, Langston skipped classes. Physics was a mystery, trigonometry "a Chinese puzzle," and French was boring. Instead of studying, he read books and went to lectures at the Rand School of Social Science and to readings at the Harlem Branch Library, where he met a fellow poet, Countee Cullen. Most often, he went to the theater. Fascinated by the hit musical *Shuffle Along,* the first Broadway show with an all-black cast, he sat at the top of the gallery and saw it over and over. And to cheer himself up, he wrote poetry:

> *Sometimes when I'm lonely,*
> *Don't know why,*
> *Keep thinkin' I won't be lonely*
> *By and by.*

Langston's private life as a poet was soon to end. A change of address on his magazine subscription alerted the editors of the *Crisis* that their mystery poet from Mexico was now at Columbia. When they invited him to lunch, Langston was "panic-stricken." How would he act meeting such intelligent, influential people? What would he say? He was so nervous he took his mother along because she loved to talk.

Jessie Fauset, the literary editor at *Crisis* who had encouraged him from the beginning, soon put him at ease with her warm manner. And his admiration overcame his awe at meeting one of his heroes: W. E. B. Du Bois, author of his favorite childhood book, *The Souls of Black*

Folk, and the man to whom Langston would dedicate his poem "The Negro Speaks of Rivers." Buoyed by their interest, Langston sent more poems to the *Crisis,* and its manager arranged Langston's first public reading of his poems, in the black Community Church. It would mark the beginning of a lifetime of readings.

Near the end of the school year, his father had a stroke and was partially paralyzed. Although Langston sent a letter of sympathy, he made no plans to visit him. Their relationship had been so antagonistic when they were together that he felt there was nothing he could do to help James Hughes.

Langston studied hard for his exams and did reasonably well, except for math and science, and he flunked physical education. But one year was enough at Columbia. Not wanting to waste his father's money, he wrote to James Hughes, whose health had improved, telling him not to send any more money. He wanted to try to be a writer. His father never replied.

With thirteen dollars to his name, the twenty-year-old poet was on his own again, free to follow his dream.

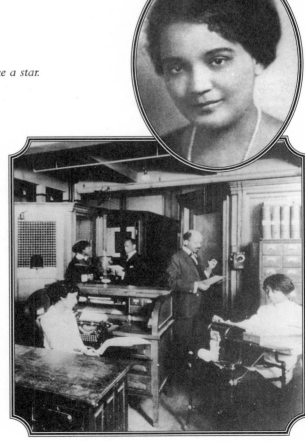

O, sweep of stars over Harlem streets,

. . . . .

Reach up your hand, dark boy, and take a star.
Out of the little breath of oblivion
　　That is night,
　　Take just
　　One star.

Jessie Fauset, 1924 (top)
W.E.B. Du Bois at work in the
Crisis office (bottom)

Langston Hughes, 1923

The Big Sea

"I didn't advertise for a colored boy." Langston heard the same words everywhere he applied for a job. He was beginning to think his father was right: that in the United States, skin color was destiny. It determined the kind of job he could get—and if he could get a job at all.

Langston finally found work on a truck farm on Staten Island. Every day from dawn until dark he labored in the fields; at night, he slept on a pile of hay in the barn. He felt useful helping to grow vegetables to feed a city. He liked it, except for the mosquitoes before dawn that "bit your ears off."

In the fall, he delivered flowers. Every box cost more than he earned in ten days. That made up his mind. If he had to work at boring jobs for low pay, why not see the world? After three weeks of hunting, he found a freighter in need of a messboy.

To his dismay, the ship was bound for nowhere. It was towed up the Hudson River and anchored at Jones Point, at the far end of a graveyard of over a hundred ships, outdated after the war. His hopes for adventure dashed, Langston oiled machinery, checked cables, and listened wistfully as other sailors told tales of the high seas and the exotic lands they had seen. Through the long, dark winter, as the creaky ship rocked in the wind and the radiator hissed, Langston holed up in the "rusty tub." He tried to look at the bright side. At least now he had plenty of time to read and to write poetry.

A few of his poems were published in the *Crisis,* and he worked all winter on a poem about a piano player he had heard in a caberet in Harlem. "There are seldom many changes in my poems once they're down," Langston would write in *The Big Sea.* "The first two or three lines come to me from something I'm thinking about, or looking at, or doing, and the rest of the poem (if there is to be a poem) flows from those first few lines, usually right away." This poem was different. He couldn't get the ending right. He kept taking "The Weary Blues" out of his suitcase to work on, unsatisfied.

Spring came, and the smell of the sea. Langston quit his job, eager to find a ship that was going somewhere. When he found a freighter bound for Africa, he quickly signed on as messboy. He was ecstatic: "Africa! The real thing, to be touched and seen, not merely read about in a book."

So long,
So far away
Is Africa.
Not even memories alive
Save those that history books create,
Save those that songs
Beat back into the blood—
Beat out of blood with words sad-sung.

On June 13, 1923, the *West Hesseltine* sailed into the open sea, its engines throbbing as it surged through the swells toward Africa. Late at night, Langston stood on the deck, sea spray blowing in his face, imagining the dark continent of his dreams. He took a big breath of salt-tangy air, leaned over the rail, and threw all his books overboard (except Walt Whitman's *Leaves of Grass*). Langston wanted to feel free of all the years he had spent reading, trying to forget his loneliness and unhappiness by living through books. Now, at twenty-one, he was free to begin a new life: "It was like throwing a million bricks out of my heart."

As he sailed down the west coast of Africa, Langston's excitement grew. Soon he would step on the golden sand of his ancestral home. Soon he would see black, beautiful people—his people.

> *I am a Negro:*
> *Black as the night is black,*
> *Black like the depths of my Africa.*

But the Africans laughed at him. "You, white man!" they called him, for his color was much lighter than theirs. "That hurt me a lot," Langston would admit. Even in the land of his ancestors, he wasn't accepted. Where *did* he belong?

From the Azores to Angola, in thirty-two ports of call, the poet sang of sun and booming surf, bright parrots, chanting black boatmen, and golden moons ripe as melons. But behind the light, darkness lurked. Langston wrote of traders with whips and guns driving natives like mules as they dragged seven-ton mahogany logs from the forest to the shore. After the logs were floated to the ship, Kru boys dived in the water to fasten them with chains. Afraid they would be crushed between the logs or caught by sharks, Langston wondered how life could be considered so cheap that someone's grand piano or furniture would be made out of human suffering and death.

Before he left Africa, Langston bought a souvenir for his "brother," Kit. He paid three shillings, an old shirt, and a pair of shoes for Jocko, a wild red monkey. Jocko bit his master every time he picked him up. When he was tamed, Jocko bit Langston every time he put him down.

After six months of storms at sea, wormy oatmeal, drunken fights, and brewing mutiny, the *West Hesseltine* sailed into New York Harbor, where the entire crew was fired.

Langston punched holes in a small black bag, packed Jocko inside, and soon boarded a train to visit his reunited family, now in Pennsylvania. The conductor sniffed, frowning, every time he walked past the sailor and his black bag. Worried that Jocko would be discovered and put off the train, Langston hoped the conductor thought it was the sailor who smelled like a zoo.

Although his family met him at the station, he didn't tell them about Jocko until they arrived home. Then he opened his black bag and Jocko jumped out, "big as the jungle." His mother screamed, Kit ran, and Homer laughed. But Jocko was too wild for Carrie. When Langston left for New York, she sold the "Congo devil" to a pet store.

The big sea beckoned again, and he signed on as messboy on a freighter bound for Holland. A storm struck the first day out, and for twenty days the ship plunged through seas twice as tall as the mast. After his second storm-battered voyage on the freighter, Langston left the ship in Rotterdam. He had decided Paris would be safer.

He reached the City of Light with seven dollars in his pocket. In the falling snow, he walked along the Seine River, gazing in wonder at places he had read about in books. Paris was as enchanting as he had imagined. When he looked for a job, however, the city soon lost its charm. Cold and hungry, he searched anxiously for a month, eating only bread and cheese once a day. But there were no jobs for foreigners.

"Before I would have written my own father for a penny, I would have died in Paris," Langston recalled years later. He was sure his father would say "You should have listened to me, and gone to Switzerland to study!"

Down to his last francs, he found work as a doorman at the Cozy Corner nightclub. It paid five francs, less than a quarter a night, but it included dinner. To look more official, Langston bought a blue military hat with gold braid at a flea market. The first night, he stuffed himself and fell asleep at his post outside the club. Fortunately, he wasn't fired. But when he found out his main job was to break up fights, he quit.

With the help of a friend, Langston got a job washing dishes at a nightclub called Le Grand Duc. He made friends with Bruce, the one-eyed cook, and Bricktop, the redheaded singer from New York who would become internationally famous. While the poet scrubbed through the night, the best jazz musicians from all over the city would drop in after hours and jam until dawn. He heard "music that would almost make your heart stand still":

> *Play it,*
> *Jazz band!*
> *You know that tune*
> *That laughs and cries at the same time.*

He experimented with his poems, trying to catch the spirit and rhythm of jazz. When he was satisfied, Langston sent his unique poems to America, where they were published in the

Crisis, *Opportunity*, and other magazines. His reputation as a poet was growing—but his income was not. No magazine had ever paid him a penny for his poetry.

After five months in Paris, Langston traveled to Italy and spent a glorious month in the sun with friends. One night, as he slept on a train, his money and passport were stolen, and he was stranded in Genoa. His only hope was to find a ship that would hire a black messboy. He waited week after week, living as a beachcomber on the edge of starvation, while ships with white crews sailed into the harbor and left without him.

One day, Langston got a job painting the sides of a ship anchored in the harbor. He didn't know how to raise or lower the scaffolding, and he didn't dare try because he couldn't swim, so he swung all day in one spot, painting the same area over and over.

Then he couldn't find another job. In desperation, Langston sat on a park bench and wrote an article about Africa, "Burutu Moon." He sent it to the *Crisis*, pleading to be paid. He waited for weeks without a word.

Finally a freighter with a colored crew sailed into the harbor—the most beautiful ship the starving poet had ever seen. The captain signed him on as a workaway, an unpaid crewman, and Langston chipped decks, scraping off old paint, and did odd jobs all the way back to the United States. He would soon find out that the *Crisis* had sent twenty dollars; it had arrived one day after he left Genoa.

He landed in New York City with a few poems and a quarter he had earned by washing the chief mate's shirt. But Langston figured his European trip was a bargain. Since he had started out in Paris with seven dollars, his ten months in Europe had cost him only six dollars and seventy-five cents.

Welcomed in Harlem as a hero, Langston discovered that his poems had made him a name in black literary circles,

The Crisis, June 1924

Hughes with Charles S. Johnson, E. Franklin Frazier, Rudolph Fisher, and Hubert Delany, May, 1925

and his wandering, adventurous life had caught people's imagination. As Countee Cullen had written to a friend, "He is really squeezing life like a lemon."

At a party given in his honor, Langston was asked if he had any new poems. With a shy smile, he pulled a worn notebook out of his pocket and began to read. In his admiring audience was another young writer, Arna Bontemps, who would become his confidant, collaborator, and closest friend.

Although Harlem was exciting, Langston had college on his mind. Now, after his travels, he felt ready. He was almost twenty-three years old and had experienced many different cultures. He wanted to understand the world and why people were the way they were. An education would help his writing, Langston believed, and his dream "to be of more use to my race."

Life is a big sea
full of many fish.
I let down my nets
and pull.

Carrie Hughes c. 1925

Sweet Blues!

Home was Washington, D.C., in November 1924. Langston called it home because his mother and Kit were living there. She was working as a maid and had separated from his stepfather again. This time for good, she said. They had moved in with her well-to-do cousins, and the poet was invited to join them. Langston had misgivings when his relatives looked askance at his shabby clothes and raised their eyebrows at the way he had traveled to Europe.

Although Langston heard praise for his poetry from cultured black society, he never heard an offer of a college scholarship. He had pinned his hopes on Howard University because his great-uncle John Mercer Langston had been the first dean of its law school in 1869, acting president of the university, and later, Congressman from Virginia. Langston also hoped that Alain Locke, a professor friend at Howard, might help. To the poet's great disappointment, his request for a scholarship was turned down.

No one offered him a good job, either. When he found work in a wet-wash laundry, his relatives were shocked. They thought it wasn't proper for a poet (or a relative) to have such a menial job. Langston's low opinion of middle-class blacks sank even lower when he saw how his relatives and others looked down on their own people who didn't have a college degree or whose skin was darker than theirs.

And his mother was treated the same snobbish way. She came crying to Langston one day, humiliated by something that her cousins had said. They moved out, to two small, unheated rooms. Langston thought it was a big improvement. Months later, Carrie would be told not to come to a banquet where her son was reading his poems, since she probably didn't have an evening gown. Angry at the insult to his mother, Langston would refuse to attend.

Working at the laundry for twelve dollars a week, he tried to save one dollar a week for college. But Kit needed shoes or his mother needed more rent money. In the bitter cold, Langston couldn't even afford an overcoat. How could he ever save for college?

Half-hungry and unhappy, he liked to hang out with the blacks down on Seventh Street, ordinary folks who worked hard for a living. Life was real there. No one put on any airs the way middle-class black society did. Langston felt at home. He listened to people's stories, laughed at their jokes, and clapped his hands to their gospel songs shouted in church. And he heard the blues, their "broke and broken-hearted" songs. "Songs folks make up when their heart hurts . . . Sad funny songs—too sad to be funny and too funny to be sad." He felt their hopes and frustrations, and "tried to write poems like the songs they sang."

There was strength in their songs, too. Langston heard the "pulse beat of the people who keep on going. Like the waves of the sea . . ."

> I've been scarred and battered.
> My hopes the wind done scattered.
> Snow has friz me, sun has baked me.
>   Looks like between 'em
>   They done tried to make me
> Stop laughin', stop lovin', stop livin'—
>   But I don't care!
>   I'm still here!

One night as he walked home, Langston sang a blues poem to himself, trying to get the words right. A man across the road rushed over and asked anxiously, "Son, are you ill?"

"No," Langston said, surprised. "Just singing."

"I thought you were groaning," he said. "Sorry!"

Langston was careful not to sing in the streets after that. But folks still sang their blues on Seventh Street. Although they could see the golden dome of the capital city of democracy, it didn't shine for them. Langston and his friends couldn't buy tickets to a new movie or stage show, or drink sodas in a restaurant outside their black ghetto.

Yet Langston wasn't bitter like his father. He remembered his grandmother giving him an apple with a brown spot on it. He didn't want to eat the apple. His grandmother had said, "What's the matter with you, boy? You can't expect every apple to be a perfect apple. . . . Bite that speck out and eat that apple, son. It's still a good apple."

Kit Clark c. 1937

That's the way the world is, Langston thought. If you bite the specks out, it's still a good apple. His belief was tested through the long winter. He got a bad cold and lost his laundry job; he broke out in a rash after eating too many oysters while working in an oyster house, so he quit; and his mother refused to feed him if he wasn't working. She told him he was wasting his time writing poetry.

After many hungry days, Langston was hired as a research assistant for Dr. Carter G. Woodson, founder of the Association for the Study of Negro Life and History. Although his relatives approved of his "position," the poet wasn't happy in an office. The work strained his eyes, and he "always liked jobs in places where you eat." At night, he'd come back to his cold home and write poetry until he felt better.

> *Well, son, I'll tell you:*
> *Life for me ain't been no crystal stair.*
> *It's had tacks in it,*
> *And splinters,*
> *And boards torn up,*
> *And places with no carpet on the floor—*
> *Bare.*
> *But all the time*
> *I'se been a-climbin' on,*
>
> *. . . . .*
>
> *So boy, don't you turn back.*

Some of his poems were published in the *Messenger*, a Socialist magazine, and ten poems were featured in a special issue of *Survey Graphic* edited by Alain Locke, celebrating the "New Negro" of the Harlem Renaissance. Langston was grateful to be published, even though magazines still didn't pay for his poetry.

After he wrote poems, Langston would put them away in a bottom drawer. In a few weeks, he would read them again: "If they seemed bad, I would throw them away." One poem that he didn't throw away, after more than two years of rereading, changed his life. "The

Weary Blues," the poem he had written on the rusty tub, won first prize in a poetry contest in May 1925. He called it his "lucky poem."

At the awards banquet in New York City, Langston collected his forty-dollar prize and celebrated with other winners, including Countee Cullen and Zora Neale Hurston. With deep satisfaction, Langston heard his prize-winning poem read in ringing tones by James Weldon Johnson, renowned poet and novelist. Among the crowd congratulating Langston was Charles S. Johnson, editor of *Opportunity* magazine, sponsor of the contest, and many young, talented writers and influential people who would become his friends.

Carl Van Vechten, a white critic and writer who was impressed with Langston's poetic gifts, became his

Opportunity Literary Contest Award Dinner

mentor. Within weeks, he found a publisher for Langston's first book, *The Weary Blues*, and wrote the introduction. He would offer advice and support, emergency loans, and loyal friendship for forty years.

From a ship bound for nowhere, Langston had cast his lucky poem, snagging a prize, his first book, and lifelong friends. His ship had set sail at last. His dream was coming true.

> *O Blues!*
> *Swaying to and fro on his rickety stool*
> *He played that sad raggy tune like a musical fool.*
> *Sweet Blues!*
> *Coming from a black man's soul.*
> *O Blues!*

At Cresson Hall, Lincoln University, 1928

On Top of the Mountain

In spite of his success, the poet's heart was still set on college. But how? Publication, though gratifying, wouldn't put much money in his pockets. Then in August, a literary contest by the *Crisis* granted his longed-for wish. Not because of the prizes he won (a disappointing second in essays and third in poetry), but the remarkable woman he met: Amy Spingarn, a wealthy amateur artist and poet, donor of the prize money. Admiring Langston's talent and spirit, she offered him financial help for college. His goal finally realized, a grateful Langston wrote that he was happier than he had been for many years.

After his dismal experience at Columbia, Langston knew he wanted to go to a black school. Lincoln University, a small college in the country near Philadelphia, Pennsylvania, was a happy choice. At the men's college, he could wear old clothes, "study and live simply," and still visit Harlem on weekends for concerts, parties, and plays.

In February 1926, Langston set out to enjoy college life. He even thought being hazed as a new student was fun: he was teased as "boy poet" and paddled until he couldn't sit down. "Lincoln is more like what home ought to be than any place I've ever seen," he wrote to Carl Van Vechten. His ready smile and fun-loving nature won Langston many friends. In his senior year, he would be voted the most popular student.

As if to make up for his lonely years, Langston enthusiastically took part in school activities. He cheered the football team at bonfire pep rallies, joined a fraternity, and dumped water out of upper-story windows on students dressed for a date. In his sophomore year, he wrote the class guilty plea for shaving freshmen's heads. As a junior, he joined the Sportsmen's Club and helped steal the chapel organ to liven up their meetings with music.

One of Langston's fellow pranksters was Thurgood Marshall, who would become the first black Supreme Court justice. High-spirited, he had a reputation as the noisiest man in the class. It was said that he'd sing and dance down the halls past midnight, banging out the beat on tin pans.

But college life was not all fun and games. Hailed by the *New York Times* as a "poet of promise," the new author was in demand for poetry readings, mainly in black churches. And in-between studies, Langston always found time to write. "A House in Taos" won first prize in a national poetry contest for undergraduates, and his poem "Youth" was published on the cover of a white magazine:

> *We have tomorrow*
> *Bright before us*
> *Like a flame.*

Challenged by the problems facing black writers, Langston was inspired to write a powerful essay, "The Negro Artist and the Racial Mountain," published in *The Nation* in June 1926. In his manifesto, Langston exhorted black writers to be proud to be black and to write about it. For "the mountain standing in the way of any true Negro art in America" was "this urge within the race toward whiteness, the desire . . . to be as little Negro and as much American as possible." Langston was only twenty-four years old, but he had laid the bedrock of his lifework.

When Langston was a sophomore, his second book of poetry was published. Its title, *Fine Clothes to the Jew*, as well as its content, were controversial. Written in the spirit of the blues, his poems told the stories of common black folk down on their luck:

Langston with Friends at Lincoln University

Homesick blues, Lawd,
'S a terrible thing to have.

. . . .

To keep from cryin'
I opens ma mouth an' laughs.

Although many white literary critics admired his "new verse form," most black reviewers were shocked. "Trash!" they wrote in disgust. He was criticized for using dialect and writing about lower-class blacks. Hughes was "a disgrace to the race," a "sewer dweller." Why didn't he write about "nice" people? Langston wasn't surprised. Their reviews reflected the same snobbish middle-class attitude he had noted among blacks in Washington, D.C..

He wrote about life as he saw it, the poet explained to a reviewer. On Seventh Street, he had seen "the ones to whom life is least kind. I try to catch the hurt of their lives. . . . They are the people I know best."

Langston was soon to meet someone to whom life was most kind—and who lived on Park

Charlotte Mason

Avenue in New York City. Charlotte Mason, a wealthy white widow in her seventies, a patron of African art, offered Langston financial and spiritual support for his creative "flight." "Godmother," as she wished to be called, seemed to be an answer to his needs. She believed in him, and Langston felt the love he had longed for as a child. He opened up his heart to her and shared his inmost feelings.

For the next two and a half years, Godmother prodded him to create and to show her all his drafts for approval. Langston was happy for a time. He loved her and treasured the many hours they spent together. And now he could write without worrying about money, go to plays, buy clothes, and eat well. But the price was steep. His novel, *Not Without Laughter*, based on his lonely childhood feelings, was painful to write, and he felt constant pressure to write on demand and to her liking. After many months, Godmother's commands for itemized accounts of his expenses chillingly reminded him of his father.

In June 1929, Langston graduated from college and struggled to finish his novel. He would never feel happy about this book, wishing he could have written it better. When at last he was done, drained and exhausted, Godmother pressured him to produce other writings. Feeling like a puppet dancing on her strings, Langston rebelled.

Her rejection sent him reeling. Afraid of losing her love and her passionate belief in him, he begged for her friendship—no money, just friendship. Cold and distant, Godmother treated him like an abandoned child. Langston's hurt turned inward, and he was violently ill, even more than he had been years ago in a Mexican hospital, when he was sick with hatred for his father.

Langston's stomach felt better and his spirits brightened when the new year of 1931 brought good news: *Not Without Laughter* had won the Harmon Gold Award for distinguished black literature. Its prize of four hundred dollars was the most money Langston had ever received for his writing.

He gave one hundred dollars to his mother, and with an artist friend, Zell Ingram, went to seek the sun in Cuba and Haiti. He needed rest and time to reflect on his future. Without a patron, the twenty-nine-year-old poet faced an unknown path.

At Port-au-Prince, Haiti's capital,

Langston in Haiti, 1931

Langston was appalled at the squalor: diseased children begging in the streets; families too poor to buy soap, living in thatched huts; barefoot people who couldn't read or write. The contrast with the wealthy upper class was too painful for Langston's sense of social justice. In protest, he would write an essay, "People Without Shoes."

Where was the legendary island that had enchanted him since he was a child? Langston wondered sadly. He remembered his grandmother's hero-stories of Haiti, where black slaves had overthrown their French rulers a century earlier. Proudly, she had recounted stories of his great-uncle John Mercer Langston, who had twice served as United States Minister to Haiti. Hoping to find inspiration at the fabled fortress at Cap-Haitien, Langston and Zell boarded a ramshackle open-air bus, sharing space with chickens and pigs, and headed for the wild north coast. Langston felt as if he was on a pilgrimage: his goal, the Citadel.

High on a mountain peak, the fortress loomed in ruins of past glory. Eagerly Langston climbed to the Citadel, symbol of black independence, the ghosts of heroes haunting the battlements. He could almost hear Dessalines's cries of freedom and Henri Christophe's triumphant epitaph: "I am reborn from my ashes" echoing in the wind-swept ruins. Overcome by emotion, Langston stood on the mountaintop overlooking the sea. The promise of tomorrow spread out shining before him, and his spirit was renewed.

He resolved to make his living by writing. But not any kind of writing: "I wanted to write seriously and as well as I knew how about the Negro people, and make *that* kind of writing earn for me a living."

Bold words—but in the real world, was it possible? No black American writer had ever done it before. Langston knew that the odds were against him. Because of his color, he couldn't get a job writing radio or movie scripts, or editing books for white publishers. Many magazines didn't pay for his stories or

Henri Christophe Citadel, Cap-Haitien, Haiti

poems, and he couldn't live on his royalties, either. His second book of poetry had not sold well. How could he make a living?

He didn't want to teach, and write on the side, as some of his friends did. And he wouldn't write stories to appeal to white readers, hiding his color behind a pen name, as others did.

Langston wore his color "like a banner for the proud." In his heart, full of his grandmother's hero-stories, he believed that if he wrote about the lives of ordinary blacks, they would know that their feelings and ideas counted, that they were important. If he gave them a sense of history, of where they came from, they would know who they were. And the truth would set them free—to dream.

We build our temples for tomorrow, strong as we know how,
and we stand on top of the mountain, free within ourselves.

Langston on Tour, 1932

I, Too, Sing America

How would he "turn poetry into bread"? Langston wondered. Fate had an answer back in the United States. Driving up the Florida coast in Zell Ingram's Ford coupe, the friends picked up a passenger in Daytona Beach. Mary McLeod Bethune, a bighearted woman with a mission, crammed into the car's single seat with Langston and Zell, and in the summer heat they headed for New York. "We'll make it," she said.

Once a barefoot cotton picker, now founder and president of a black junior college, Bethune would become education advisor to five presidents of the United States. She was so popular in the South people said that chickens would fly off in a panic when she came their way. They knew that necks would be wrung in her honor and fried chicken would be served. To their delight, Langston and Zell were well fed on their journey.

Bethune encouraged Langston to tour the South reading his poems. "People need poetry," she told him. She was persuasive. Here was his chance to bring poetry to the people he had written it for, and perhaps make a living at it.

Jim Crow sign

Soon after he reached New York, Langston applied for a grant from the Rosenwald Fund. In a letter to Walter White he stated his goals: to create interest in the works of black writers and "do what I can to encourage young literary talent among our people."

His friends thought he was crazy. Who would pay to hear him in the poor South? Especially during the Depression, when millions were out of work and out of hope, homeless and hungry. Langston was determined to try. He wrote to all the black colleges, offering to speak for a fee of one hundred dollars. If a school couldn't pay, he suggested fifty, then a sliding fee, down to whatever the college could afford. At free, he had many takers.

To make his poetry affordable to everyone, he and a white artist, Prentiss Taylor, founded the Golden Stair Press in Taylor's home. With a loan from Carl Van Vechten, they published a small booklet of poems, *The Negro Mother*, written in simple language about subjects Langston believed would appeal to southern blacks.

His grant money paid for trip expenses and a Model A Ford sedan. Since the poet didn't know how to drive, he asked college friend Radcliffe Lucas to be his driver, offering to share any profits with him. Lucas quickly accepted, and Langston called him his "business manager."

Before dawn on November 2, 1931, they loaded the Ford with an exhibit of books by black writers, posters to advertise the readings, and Langston's poems to sell: booklets for a quarter, single-poem broadsides for a dime, and a special one-dollar edition of *The Weary Blues*. Then they set out for the South:

Dark ones of Africa,
I bring you my songs
To sing on the Georgia roads.

They toured for five months down dusty roads, past hotels and restaurants posting WHITES ONLY signs; past gas-station rest rooms marked MEN AND LADIES—and single shanties out back marked COLORED. Langston and Raddie had no choice but to eat and sleep in the homes of neighborly blacks along the way.

One day, in Virginia, they stopped at a café to buy cold sodas. When the owner saw them, he held the door shut and yelled, "We got a hole cut for you-all people on the side!" Langston and Raddie walked around the building and saw a hole in the wall marked COLORED. They left, thirsty.

At the University of North Carolina, the only white school on the tour, protesters threatened to run Langston out of town, and police stood guard outside the hall where he was reading. In Mississippi, he was warned not to read his poems or sell his books, and was also reminded that there were twelve lynchings in the past year.

But danger didn't stop Langston. At every opportunity, he spoke out against injustice, including the controversial Scottsboro trial, and read poems that struck at the heart of the South's racial prejudice. Thousands of students heard him in every state in the South, and he learned that "poetry can mean something to uneducated people. Even in the backwoods, they seemed to know what I was talking about, and to appreciate it."

Colored and White Water Fountains

Throughout his life, Langston would bring his poetry to the people, crossing America by train in the segregated Jim Crow car. His tours were exhausting: seventeen states, one season. They took time and energy away from his writing, but they paid the bills. And reflected back from the faces of his people was their gift of acceptance and love.

Langston would read from his poetry book for children, *The Dream Keeper*, published in 1932, and from favorite poems he had pasted on its blank pages and written inside its covers in his large, flowing handwriting.

Sometimes he read poems to a blues or jazz background. Nobody had ever done that before. In the 1920s, he had read with Fats Waller at the piano in Harlem homes and with a saxophone and piano at college. In the 1950s, he would read poetry on television, backed by jazz pianist Billy Taylor; record an album, *The Weary Blues*, with the Charles Mingus quintet; and perform poetry-to-jazz sessions in Greenwich Village. And in 1960, he would read poems set to the blues at the Newport Jazz Festival, where he was a director.

In his long 1961 poem *Ask Your Mama: Twelve Moods for Jazz*, Langston's love spilled over in the margins, where he wrote musical cues for a jazz ensemble. He was called the "original jazz poet," this music-loving man who couldn't carry a tune. Yet the music in his poetry resonated in the hearts of those who heard him read.

Langston liked to end his readings with one of his favorite poems, his dream of the future:

> *I, too, sing America.*
>
> *I am the darker brother.*
> *They send me to eat in the kitchen*
> *When company comes,*
> *But I laugh,*
> *And eat well,*
> *And grow strong.*

Aboard the Europa, 1932

I Dream a World

In June 1932, Langston jumped at the chance to make a movie in Russia. A Soviet film company hired twenty-two black artists for a movie about race and labor relations in the United States. Langston was to write the dialogue.

Rushing cross-country by car from a poetry-reading tour in California to a pier in New York, Langston was the last one up the *Europa*'s gangplank. Horns blared a midnight sailing as he hustled aboard, lugging his bags and his constant traveling companions: a typewriter, a Victrola, and a box of blues and jazz records. He was eager to see the country whose revolution had kindled his idealism at Central High.

Although the group was entertained royally, *Black and White* was doomed from the start. The Soviet script was so unrealistic in its portrayal of American race relations that Langston, if he hadn't wanted to laugh, would have cried. Ineptness and politics combined to ensure that the movie was never made. Langston, however, stayed on in the Soviet Union.

He liked the way he was treated—as an equal—and he

Kolya Shagurin, Langston Hughes, Shaarieh Kikilov, and Arthur Koestler in Central Asia, 1932

made a good living as a writer, a new experience for him. Hired by *Izvestia*, he toured Central Asia writing articles about ethnic minorities; *Not Without Laughter* was translated into Russian (*Smech Skvoz Slezy*) and his poetry into Uzbek; and his revolutionary poems were published in *New Masses* and *International Literature*. Seen through his eyes, a country that had outlawed racism offered hope for a better world:

> *Good morning, Revolution:*
> *You're the very best friend*
> *I ever had.*
> *We gonna pal around together from now on.*

But the friendship didn't last. In later years, as repression of rights grew under Communist rule, disillusionment would set in for Langston and many other radicals.

After a year his travel permit expired, and Langston packed up memories of a budding romance with Sylvia Chen, an Afro-Chinese dancer, and headed for Japan via the Trans-Siberian Express. He traveled to China and sailed across the Pacific to California, ready to rest his itchy feet. Many years later, he would describe his round-the-world adventures in his second autobiography, *I Wonder As I Wander.*

At Carmel-by-the-Sea, in a cottage loaned to him by a new friend, Noël Sullivan, Langston found a quiet retreat where he could devote himself to writing, "unworried and unhurried." Sullivan, a spiritual man who used his wealth to encourage artistic and humanitarian causes, would remain a devoted, trusted friend. Warmed by the sun and Sullivan's generous heart, Langston set a goal of writing one short story a week until he had enough for a book. He worked ten to twelve hours a day with a break in the afternoon to walk on the beach with Greta, Sullivan's German shepherd. Weekends were filled with friends and parties, brimming with good food, stimulating talk, and laughter.

He had an agent now, and Maxim Lieber was imaginative. He sold some of Langston's stories to major white magazines, including *Esquire, Scribner's,* and *The New Yorker,* a first for black writers in the 1900s. Langston sent most of his earnings to his mother in Oberlin, Ohio, but she complained in every letter that he didn't send enough. She thought he was rich now that he was a published author. When he told her he could barely support himself, Carrie retorted, "You ought to quit writing, and get a job with a steady income."

On his thirty-second birthday, Langston celebrated happily with Noël Sullivan and the poet Robinson Jeffers and his wife, Una, at a picnic in the brooding hills of Big Sur, high above the Pacific. His new book of short stories, *The Ways of White Folks*, gratefully dedicated to Sullivan, would soon be published to good reviews. His future seemed as unlimited as the far horizon.

But storm clouds were gathering in the sunny skies of California in 1934. Caught up in the wave of radical causes sweeping the state, Langston wrote social protest poems and a book about his year in the Soviet Union. His publisher curtly rejected them. Months later, the Theatre Guild would turn down his collaborative play with Ella Winter, *Blood on the Fields*, based on a cotton workers' strike. Langston's confidence in his career was crumbling.

As dock strikes paralyzed the state, Langston joined his friends in the local John Reed Club, supporting strikers—from longshoremen to farm workers. With journalist Lincoln

Steffens, Marie Short, and others, he gave speeches, raised money, and collected clothes and food for the striking workers. Then the mood of Carmel turned ugly. Communists were blamed for causing the strikes, and the John Reed Club was a prime target. Armed vigilantes roamed the streets, and Langston was warned that his life was in danger.

He fled to Reno, Nevada, where no one knew him and he could write in peace. Desperate for money, his bank account overdrawn by $5.80, Langston applied for a Guggenheim fellowship. Then he sat down at his typewriter and wrote short stories about whites under a pen name—something he had once scorned doing.

Troubled one day, thinking of his father, he wrote a short story called "Mailbox for the Dead." Two weeks later, a letter came with news of his father's death on October 22nd—the very day Langston had written the story.

He borrowed money to travel to Mexico, but his hopes of a legacy, if he had any, proved to be empty. As if his son had never existed, James Hughes didn't even mention Langston's name in his will. Later, in Hughes's files, Langston found all the letters he had written to his father. If he felt any pang of regret or loss, Langston never showed it.

Drifting, uncertain about his future, he stayed in Mexico until he could make enough money to leave. He wrote "white" short stories, but his heart wasn't in it, and his agent had trouble selling them. Langston was more enthused about translating Mexican and Cuban writers for free and trying to get them published in the United States. And Mexico wasn't all work. Langston joined a hiking club and went to the bullfights. Years later, writing about his bohemian days living in a shack with Mexican poet Andres Henestrosa and French photographer Henri Cartier-Bresson, Langston couldn't remember when he "had more fun with less cash."

After six months, good news knocked on Langston's door. He had been awarded the Guggenheim fellowship, and its money would buy him time to write. Langston was ready to move on, eager to write seriously again. His first stop was Los Angeles to work on a children's book with his best friend, Arna Bontemps. Their 1931 collaboration, *Popo and Fifina*, a children's story set in Haiti, had been a success. Now they hoped to write a story set in Mexico.

Arna's children were happy whenever Langston came to visit. They loved him like a favorite uncle, for he laughed a lot and always brought them presents. Over the years, the writer friends would exchange almost twenty-three hundred letters with gossipy news, messages of support, and ideas for future projects—most of which would never be published. Although Langston trusted Arna like a brother, he never dropped his breezy tone to write about his inner feelings. As in his autobiographies, Langston skimmed the surface of his life in his letters and left the depths to be discovered in his poetry.

In September 1935, after an absence of three years, Langston decided to join his mother and Kit in Oberlin. Her letters had been disturbing. Out of money, sick, and afraid to go to the doctor, she begged him to come home. "Dear heart," she wrote pitifully, "I have been so lonely!" Homer Clark, who had reappeared, had performed his vanishing act again and twenty-three-year-old Kit still didn't have a job. Within a month of Langston's stay, his mother would be diagnosed with breast cancer. It wouldn't take long before her medical expenses and Kit's college tuition would drain most of Langston's Guggenheim fellowship money.

For the next two years, the poet scratched out a living lecturing and writing, scattering his talents across the country. In Cleveland, his old Playground House, now a theater called Karamu House, brought back warm memories. Rowena and Russell Jelliffe, who had befriended Langston as a lonely high school student, hired him as resident playwright for the Gilpin Players.

Returning to his racial themes, Langston wrote comedies based on black folklore, and the vitality of his voice was revived. Remembering the hero-stories of Haiti, he wrote a tragedy, *Troubled Island*. His play would become a libretto for an opera with music by William Grant Still. After years of struggle, it would finally be staged in New York in 1949: the first opera written by blacks and produced by a major company in the United States.

In July 1936, the tragic drama of the Spanish Civil War took center stage. As the world watched, sparks that would set World War II afire were glowing in the wings. The cast of thousands included the Spanish army, led by General Francisco Franco, who had rebelled against the elected republican Loyalist government; Italy and Nazi Germany, who sent tanks and planes to help Franco and the fascist Nationalists; the Soviet Union, alone among the major powers, who supported the Loyalists; and from fifty-three countries, socialists, radicals, and idealists who rallied to defend the Spanish people against the Fascists, banding together to fight in the International Brigades.

Swept along in the stream of writers passionate to support Spain's heroic struggle, thirty-five-year old Langston made a will, left money for his mother, and packed up his typewriter, Victrola, and records. In June 1937, he sailed across the Atlantic to cover the war as foreign correspondent for the *Baltimore Afro-American* and *Cleveland Call and Post*.

He landed in Paris. In an ardent speech at the International Writers' Congress, Langston spoke out against racism, explaining why black volunteers would risk their lives for a land of strangers: "We Negroes of America are tired of a world in which it is possible for any one group of people to say to another: 'You have no right to happiness or freedom.'"

> *In some lands*
> *Dark night*
> *And cold steel*
> *Prevail—*
> *But the dream*
> *Will come back,*
> *And the song*
> *Break*
> *Its jail.*

To add his voice to the song of liberty, Langston crossed the border to Spain. "I thought I might not live long," he confessed. Air raids in Barcelona greeted him with eerie sirens wailing in the night. His room in Madrid, on the top floor of the Alianza mansion, had a wonderful view—of the enemy guns. He heard birds cheep-cheeping as he walked on a country road near the front: sniper bullets whistling by, he was told later. He wasn't as lucky in the city streets. Snipers opened fire, and a bullet nicked his arm.

One night, as shells whistled overhead, a booming *crash!* across the street sent Langston bolting from his typewriter to seek shelter. To drown out the sound of explosions "like a million giant firecrackers," he played his Jimmie Lunceford record, "Organ Grinder's Swing," full blast until dawn.

But daily life went on. Children still ran around in the streets, collecting shrapnel and playing hide-and-seek in the shell holes. And Langston wrote about a little girl in a starched dress, her hair braided neatly, playing scales on a piano—the living room wall a gaping hole, the top of the piano blown off. A shell had hit her house the night before, but she had to practice: "Today's the day my music teacher comes."

When force couldn't break the will of the Spanish people, the Fascists tried to starve them out. Much as he loved food, Langston was grateful to have a handful of steamed snails for dinner or a few garbanzo beans sitting lonely on a plate. "I might get hungry there," Langston would admit, "but I never got bored."

During his five-month stay in Spain, Langston wrote articles for *The Volunteer for Liberty*, translated *Gypsy Ballads* by Federico García Lorca, the Spanish poet executed by the Fascists, and broadcast news on the shortwave radio. He reported human-interest stories of the volunteer American battalion where, for the first time, blacks and whites fought side by side, in the John Brown Battery and the Abraham Lincoln Brigade: "In my heart, I salute them."

Langston with Two Members of the Abraham Lincoln Brigade, 1937

Inspired by the idealism of those who fought in the International Brigades and the heroism and resiliency of the Spanish people, Langston wrote poems about the human spirit yearning to be free, the dream of people everywhere.

I *dream a world where man*
No other man will scorn,
Where love will bless the earth
And peace its path adorn.
I dream a world where all
Will know sweet freedom's way,

. . . .

Of such I dream—
Our world!

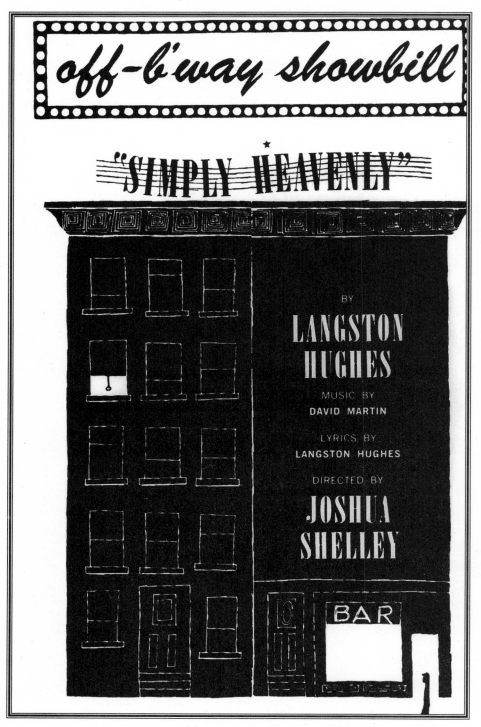

"Simply Heavenly," First Performed August 20, 1957 at the Playhouse Theater

The Dream Keeper

Back in New York, his creative energies recharged by his experiences in Spain, Langston was eager to try something new. He remembered the theater-in-the-round he had seen in Moscow, using no stage, curtain, or sets. Why not in Harlem?

With a loan from the Authors' League Fund, and the help of a radical friend, Louise Thompson, to find a space, the Harlem Suitcase Theatre was born in a second-floor loft on 125th Street. Langston wrote a long one-act play, *Don't You Want to be Free?*, a poetry play with "Singing, Music and Dancing"—a form uniquely his. Tickets cost thirty-five cents so working-class people could afford them. On April 21, 1938, to the tune of the blues on a rickety piano, his play opened to a packed house. It was a hit.

Encouraged by his success, Langston later founded black theaters in Los Angeles and Chicago. Though he made little money on his plays—only forty dollars in royalties for two hundred performances—he believed that the theaters were crucial to develop true black drama, for now other playwrights would have a chance to show their work.

Before his play opened, Langston learned that his mother was dying, and brought her from Ohio to live with him. Carrie, who had shared her love of the theater—and little else—with her son, died on June 3, 1938. If Langston grieved, he kept his feelings private.

Whatever family life Langston had was unraveling. Homer would never resurface, and Kit continued to be a problem. He had flunked out of college twice and boasted that he "had lots of fun in the process." Langston, who always called Kit his brother, helped him whenever he was in need, but he couldn't turn Kit from his self-destructive path. He would become more irresponsible and dissolute, ending up an alcoholic.

On December 7, 1941, the flames of World War II spread to the United States. The Fascist victory in Spain had been only a dress rehearsal. Langston again fought for freedom with his words, determined to fight on two fronts: against enemies abroad and against racism at home. He churned out jingles for war bond drives ("Invest a dollar to make Hitler holler") and blues lyrics for freedom rallies ("Go-and-Get-the-Enemy Blues"). And he gave rousing speeches against segregation in the armed forces; wrote "Brothers," a radio script about racial equality; and lyrics for "Freedom Road," a song for black soldiers.

When Langston turned forty-one, "Homesick Blues" was his theme song. After years of picking up his life and putting it down in rented rooms on both coasts and in cities in-between, he was weary of wandering. Travel, with its stimuli of new places, people, and ideas, would always fuel his imagination and his art; yet he hungered for a home base. In longtime friends "Aunt" Toy and "Uncle" Emerson Harper, he found his family. Once a snake charmer in a circus, now a costume designer, "Aunt" Toy loved Langston like a son. "Uncle" Emerson, a gentle, amiable musician, had set the poet's patriotic lyrics to music. They welcomed Langston with open arms, and he moved in with them. Where else but in Harlem?

On Lenox Avenue and in crowded tenements, Langston heard "the boogie-woogie rumble / of a dream deferred": people struggling to make a living, without hope for the future, "laughing to keep from crying." Out of the everyday life he saw around him, Langston wove people's stories, and wrapped their dreams in poetry.

In a neighborhood bar in 1943, he met a man who inspired the creation of Jesse B. Semple, "Simple" for short: a folk character who spoke his mind about life and discrimination with ironic humor. "Just me talking to myself," Langston explained. Simple would appear in his *Chicago Defender* newspaper column, five books, and a musical on Broadway, *Simply Heavenly*.

Inspiration also came from the riches of the past. Langston kept "drawing from the well of the past buckets of water in which to catch stars." His well was deep. He drew on black folklore and humor, on gospel songs and blues, on history and heroes. He filled his bucket to the brim.

Langston juggled many projects at the same time, writing at night so he wouldn't be disturbed, then sleeping until noon. He hired a

Christmas Greeting, 1965

secretary to help, paying him a percentage of the profits of the works they published. Each work was color-coded: typed on a different-colored paper and stacked in piles on a long table. "I am running a literary factory right now with three assembly lines going," he wrote in anguish to Arna Bontemps. Overburdened with commitments, often behind on deadlines, Langston had to work fast, and some of his writing suffered as a result.

He worked so hard because he needed the money. His books didn't sell many copies, and the theater gave him more problems than profits. He advised James Baldwin, a writer friend, "If you want to die, be disturbed, maladjusted, neurotic and psychotic, disappointed and disjointed, just write plays! Go ahead!"

The chill of censorship threatened Langston's livelihood during the "Red Scare" of the 1950s. In the anti-Communist hysteria, books were banned; writers were blacklisted, unable

The Dream Keeper

to get work; and people were jailed for refusing to testify against others. Because Langston had published radical poems in the past, had lived in the Soviet Union, and had been a member of the John Reed Club, his record was suspect.

In March 1953, Langston was summoned before Senator Joseph McCarthy's Permanent Sub-Committee on Investigations. He testified that he had never been a member of the Communist party and eloquently defended an artist's right to freedom of expression. As Langston had told Arthur Koestler, a writer friend in his Soviet Union days: he couldn't join the Communist party because he had to be free to write what was true for him, without taking orders from anyone.

No charges were made by the committee, but the damage was done. Painted by the wide brush of innuendo, his character was smeared and his career crippled. At his poetry-reading tours, protestors carried signs saying TRAITOR! Lectures were canceled and book sales dwindled. Langston described his feelings about censorship in the last lines of his poem "Un-American Investigators":

> *The committee shivers*
> *With delight in*
> *Its manure.*

Battle-weary, he faced another struggle in the mid-1950s and 1960s: the fight for civil rights. Although he supported the movement with speeches and writings, he never joined the protests and freedom marches, and was criticized for standing on the sidelines.

Perhaps he felt out of step with the times. Saddened by the bitterness and militancy sweeping the black community, Langston stopped writing about Simple in his newspaper column. For twenty-three years, he had fought prejudice with Simple's ironic humor. Now he felt that Simple could no longer speak for blacks. It was time to pass on Lewis Leary's freedom shawl to the younger generation.

When the poet at last wrote his rallying cry for the civil rights movement, public vindication came too late for Langston. *The Panther and the Lash: Poems of Our Times*, his final book of poetry, was published after he died.

At age fifty-eight, Langston Hughes was awarded the honor that meant the most to him:

At the Spingarn Medal Award Ceremony, 1960. Behind Hughes, Arthur B. Spingarn

the Spingarn Medal given by the National Association for the Advancement of Colored People. He accepted it humbly in the name of his people:

> Without them . . . there would have been no poems; without their hopes and fears and dreams, no stories; without their struggles, no dramas; without their music, no songs.

In his struggles, Langston helped "break through the wall" between blacks and their dreams: he was the first black to tour on the white lecture circuit; the first black in the United States to be admitted to PEN, the international writers' organization; the second black to be elected to the National Institute of Arts and Letters, one of the highest honors an artist in the United States can attain; and in the 1960s, he traveled to Europe and Africa as cultural emissary for the U.S. State Department.

Although he published forty-six books, edited eight others, wrote over twenty theatrical works and scores of song lyrics, was translated into every major language and awarded many honors, Langston lived in poverty most of his life. "Fame is lovely—but hard to eat," he confided to Arna Bontemps.

Loyal friends helped him in need, and he in turn helped hundreds of writers. He edited anthologies of works of new writers; he translated poems by Haitian, Cuban, Mexican, Chilean, Spanish, Russian, French, and African poets and tried to get them published. And he gave away countless books, signed in his hallmark "electric green ink." More books than he sold, he wrote Arna Bontemps. Instead of a royalty check, his publisher would send him a bill.

Generous with his time and encouragement, Langston delighted in discovering and nurturing young talent. He published Alice Walker's first short story and encouraged Gwendolyn Brooks, the future Pulitzer Prize-winning poet, when she was sixteen. To the poet Mari Evans, Langston gave a precious gift: "He made me feel that my work was worthwhile."

Friends took the place of family as Langston remained "married to his work." For his last twenty-five years, he lived with the Harpers among his extended family, the black community in Harlem.

The "poet laureate" lived as he wrote, with vitality. People always knew when Langston was in a room. They heard his laugh—an infectious, feel-fine laugh that bubbled up like a natural spring inside him. Wherever he wandered, people were drawn to his warm, easygoing charm—a warmth seasoned with humor and a zest for living that he shared with hundreds of friends.

Yet, for all his outgoing ways, he kept a part of himself to himself. "He was always smiling, always good-humored," his lifelong friend Henri Cartier-Bresson said, echoing the feelings of many who knew Langston, "even if you could sense that he kept something in reserve."

His old friend Sartur Andrzejewski caught that core of reserve when he heard Langston read his poetry years after their high school days. "I liked that you on the platform," he wrote Langston, "that you which you had never shown us before. You wear a mask so you can keep that you for work."

He "used charm as a mask," said his former secretary, George Bass. And behind the mask was the keeper of dreams.

Bring me all of your dreams,
You dreamers,
Bring me all of your
Heart melodies
That I may wrap them
In a blue cloud-cloth
Away from the too-rough fingers
Of the world.

Langston Hughes—Black History Week, Atlanta, 1947

Hold Fast To Dreams

Langston remembered the summer nights so long ago when the sound of his grandmother's voice rose and fell to the rhythm of her rocker, when out of her stories heroes followed their dreams. Children need heroes, Langston believed, and wrote histories and biographies for children.

He remembered the hurt of his childhood, and wrote a novel and autobiographies. Short stories, plays, and poetry came right out of his own life. "You will find the whole world just outside your doorstep," he told students. "You will find the world in your own eyes, if they learn how to see, in your heart if it learns how to feel."

In his heart, Langston knew who he was and where he came from. His left-lonesome childhood had left a scar that he never let anyone come close enough to see. Yet that same childhood gave him a heart full of stories; it was the source of his pride in the black race and the wellspring of his writings.

Without a loving family of his own, Langston Hughes joined the vast family out of the black past "from Africa to Georgia," singing "sorrow songs" down the freedom road. Along the way, he held out his hands to all those standing on the sidelines without a song to sing—and gave them voice.

> To fling my arms wide
> In some place of the sun,
> To whirl and to dance
> Till the white day is done.
> Then rest at cool evening
> Beneath a tall tree
> While night comes on gently,
>   Dark like me—
> That is my dream!

Night came to Langston Hughes on May 22, 1967, when he died in a New York City hospital, alone. His beloved blues and jazz were played at his funeral to celebrate his memory, for his words would keep the dream alive.

Hold fast to dreams
For if dreams die
Life is a broken-winged bird
That cannot fly.

Clay Model of Statue of Langston Hughes by James Patti

Hold Fast To Dreams

Words by
Langston Hughes

Music by
Audrey Osofsky

Hold fast to dreams___ For if dreams die___ Life is a bro-ken-winged bird That can-not fly.___ Hold fast to dreams___ For when dreams go___ Life is a bar-ren field Fro-zen with snow.___ Hold fast to dreams.___

ACKNOWLEDGMENTS AND CREDITS

For inspiration, I am grateful to Mary Sanders, who introduced me to the poetry of Hughes; my son Luther, who urged me to "do something with my song;" the memory of George Houston Bass, who told me he "believed in my work;" and Langston Hughes, whose words sustained me through twenty years: to hold fast to my dream.

My thanks also to the staff at Beinecke Rare Book and Manuscript Library at Yale University; Steve Jansen, director of the Watkins Community Museum of History, Lawrence, Kansas, where I saw James Patti's statue of Langston as a boy; and to the many other people who kindly contributed to my research.

Special thanks to Charles Dennis for his help with photo research ("a labor of love"); Judit Bodnar and Melanie Donovan, my editors; Rachel Simon, art director; and Susan Pearson, who kept her faith in the book through many years.

The photographs and prints in this book are from the following sources and are used with permission:

The *Crisis* Magazine, NAACP: pages 43, 49 (bottom), 55, 93; George Eastman House: pages 2, 50; Donna Van Der Zee: page 46; James Weldon Johnson Memorial Collection, Beinecke Rare Book and Manuscript Library, Yale University: pages 10, 16, 20, 26, 28, 32, 34, 35, 56, 58, 61, 64, 67, 68, 69, 72, 78, 80, 85, 91, 96; Lawrence Daily World: page 23; Moorland-Spingarn Research Center, Howard University: pages 49 (top), 63; James Patti: page 98; Picture Collection, Mid-Manhattan Library, New York Public Library: page 70; Schomburg Center for Research in Black Culture, New York Public Library: pages 13, 74, 75; Topeka Public Library: page 14; Special Collections/Rare Books, Wilson Library, University of Minnesota: page 88; Western Reserve Historical Society: pages 29, 36, 40.

The quotations from copyrighted works in this book are from the following sources:

Reprinted by permission of Hill & Wang, a division of Farrar, Straus & Giroux, Inc. and Harold Ober Associates Inc.:
Excerpts from *The Big Sea* by Langston Hughes. Copyright © 1940 by Langston Hughes, renewed © 1968 by Arna Bontemps and George Houston Bass.
Excerpts from *I Wonder As I Wander* by Langston Hughes. Copyright © 1956 by Langston Hughes, renewed © 1984 by George Houston Bass.
Excerpts from *Simple's Uncle Sam* by Langston Hughes. Copyright © 1965 by Langston Hughes, renewed © 1993 by Arnold Rampersad and Ramona Bass.

Reprinted by permission of Alfred A. Knopf, Inc. and Harold Ober Associates Inc.:
"The Dream Keeper," "Dreams," and lines from "Youth" from *The Dream Keeper and other poems* by Langston Hughes. Copyright © 1932 by Alfred A. Knopf, Inc., and renewed 1960 by Langston Hughes.
Lines of poetry from *Fine Clothes to the Jew* by Langston Hughes. Published 1927 by Alfred A. Knopf, Inc.
Lines from "Oppression" from *Fields of Wonder* by Langston Hughes. Copyright © 1947 by Langston Hughes.
Lines from "Color" and "Un-American Investigators" from *The Panther and the Lash* by Langston Hughes. Copyright © 1967 by Arna Bontemps and George Houston Bass.
"Hope" Copyright © 1942 by Alfred A. Knopf, Inc., and renewed 1970 by Arna Bontemps and George Houston Bass; "Still Here" Copyright © 1948 by Alfred A. Knopf, Inc., and renewed 1967 by Langston Hughes; "Dream Dust" Copyright © 1947 by Langston Hughes; and lines of poetry: reprinted from *Selected Poems* by Langston Hughes, Copyright © 1959 by Langston Hughes.

Excerpts from previously unpublished letters and papers of Langston Hughes are reprinted by arrangement with Harold Ober Associates Inc. Copyright © by Arnold Rampersad and Ramona Bass, administrators c.t.a. of the Estate of Langston Hughes. Lines of poetry from "I Dream a World," Copyright © 1945 by Langston Hughes; "To You;" and "Good Morning Revolution;" and excerpts from previously published letters are reprinted by permission of Harold Ober Associates Inc. and the Estate of Langston Hughes.

Excerpts from "The Negro Artist and the Racial Mountain" by Langston Hughes, *The Nation* magazine. Copyright © 1926 by The Nation Company, Inc. Reprinted with permission.

Excerpts from *Phylon*: "Simple and Me," by Langston Hughes, Copyright © 1945 by Clark Atlanta University, Atlanta, Georgia, and "Songs Called the Blues," by Langston Hughes, Copyright © 1941 by Clark Atlanta University, Atlanta, Georgia. Reprinted with permission.

Notes

All quotations in this book are from Langston Hughes's writings and from other documented sources. Pages where quotations may be found in Hughes's autobiographies, *The Big Sea* and *I Wonder As I Wander*, are cited at the beginning of the notes for each chapter. Other sources are credited in order of their appearance. See the Selected Bibliography for full information about a source.

Abbreviations

LH Langston Hughes

LHP Langston Hughes Papers, Yale Collection of American Literature, James Weldon Johnson Collection, Beinecke Rare Book and Manuscript Library, Yale University

Dedication

LH, "To You," *Good Morning Revolution,* ed. Berry, 171. Fisk University Library Special Collections.

Epigraph

LH, "Dreams," *The Dream Keeper*, 7.

In the Beginning, the Dream

Page 9   "Black slaves . . . mighty river": LH, "Aunt Sue's Stories," *Selected Poems of LH,* 6.

"Aunt Sue has a head full of stories": Ibid.

1. Passed-Around Child

Quotations not credited in this chapter are from LH, *The Big Sea,* pages 14, 16, 17, 26.

Page 11   "left-lonesome feeling": LH, *Simple's Uncle Sam,* 16.

Page 13   "monkey-stove": a type of parlor heater; also called "dwarf" stove.

Page 14   "You don't want to eat these": fragment in LH, "I Wonder As I Wander," LHP 519.

"who have small minds": LH, *Life Makes Poetry* recording. Kansas Collection, University of Kansas Libraries.

Page 17   "deep thinker" and "a dreamy little boy": Rampersad, *Life of LH,* 1:13.

"Catch it! Catch it!": personal papers, LHP 863.

Page 17   "She kept him": Cited in Sutton, "Langston in Lawrence," 5. Reprinted with permission of Diana Sutton Van Cleve.

Page 18   "I were a passed-around child": LH, *Simple's Uncle Sam,* 15.

2. A Bright Bowl of Brass

Quotations from LH, *The Big Sea,* 18, 22.

Page 22   "The Journal knows": Lawrence *Daily Journal,* 17 August 1910, 1. Cited in Scott, "LH of Kansas," 15.

"Your people can't come anymore": LH, "I Wonder As I Wander," LHP 519.

Page 23   "Nigger Heaven": Rampersad, *Life of LH,* 1:8.

Page 24   "Teacher's got a Jim Crow row"; "He wouldn't budge an inch"; "He always carried a smile"; "We didn't think too much about it"; "Poetry was his hobby"; "He was a bad combination"; "*A* student"; "tops in the class": Sutton, "Langston in Lawrence," 12-24.

Page 25   "Clean the spittoons, boy!": LH, "Brass Spittoons," *The Big Sea,* 264.

3. Handful of Dream Dust

Quotations from LH, *The Big Sea,* 24, 34, 56, 151.

Page 29   "The mills": LH, "Steel Mills," *The Big Sea,* 29.

"travelin' blues": LH, *Not Without Laughter,* 137.

Page 30   "as though a sudden dragon": LH, *Not Without Laughter,* 308.

"What kind of job": LH, *I Wonder As I Wander,* 308.

"Gather out of star-dust": LH, "Dream Dust," *Selected Poems,* 75.

4. Deep like the Rivers

Quotations from LH, *The Big Sea,* 35, 36, 38, 41, 45, 52, 53, 54, 62.

Page 33   "all land to the peasants": John Reed, *Ten Days That Shook the World* (New York: Bantam Classic, 1987) 1.

Page 36   "LH is crazy about 'eats'"; "soulful eyes": Rampersad, *Life of LH,* 1:33; 1:36.

Page 37   "main ambition": Rampersad, *Life of LH,* 1:36.

"When Susanna Jones wears red": LH, "When Sue Wears Red," *Selected Poems,* 68.

Page 38   "I've known rivers": LH, "The Negro Speaks of Rivers," *Selected Poems,* 4.

5. One-Way Ticket

Quotations from LH, *The Big Sea,* 59, 60, 61, 66, 72.

Page 43   "Take Harlem's heartbeat": LH, "Juke Box Love Song," *Selected Poems,* 227.

Page 44   "I pick up my life": LH, "One-Way Ticket," *Selected Poems,* 177.

6. Stars over Harlem

Quotations from LH, *The Big Sea,* 81, 84, 93.

Page 47   "When for years, I had been seeking": LH, "Aesthete in Harlem," *Opportunity,* June 1930, 182. Reprinted with permission of the National Urban League, Inc.

Page 48   "Sometimes when I'm lonely": LH, "Hope," *Selected Poems,* 35.

Page 49   "O, sweep of stars over Harlem streets": LH, "Stars", *Selected Poems,* 188.

7. The Big Sea

Quotations from LH, *The Big Sea,* 10, 11, 56, 86, 87, 91, 98, 103, 134, 137, 151, 162.

Page 52   "So long": LH, "Afro-American Fragment," *Selected Poems,* 3.

West Hesseltine: Rampersad, *Life of LH* 1:405, see notes to p. 76; LH names the ship S. S. *Malone* in *The Big Sea.* An explanation for this discrepancy and others (including dates) might be found in a letter of LH's to Arna Bontemps: he was writing his autobiography by memory because his publisher didn't pay him enough to take the time to check all the facts.

Page 53   "I am a Negro": LH, "Negro," *Selected Poems,* 8.

Page 54   "Play it, / Jazz band!": LH, "Jazz Band in a Parisian Cabaret," *Fine Clothes to the Jew,* 74.

Page 57   "He is really squeezing life": Countee Cullen to Harold Jackman, 20 July 1923. Atlanta University Center, Robert W. Woodruff Library, Archives and Special Collections. Reprinted with permission.

"to be of more use": Rampersad, *Life of LH,* 1:116.

"Life is a big sea": LH, *The Big Sea,* epigraph.

8. Sweet Blues!

Quotations from LH, *The Big Sea,* 209, 215, 216, 217.

Page 60   "broke and broken-hearted . . . too funny to be sad": LH, "Songs Called the Blues," *Phylon* 2 (Summer 1941): 143.

"I've been scarred and battered": LH, "Still Here," *Selected Poems,* 123.

Page 61   "What's the matter": LH, *I Wonder As I Wander,* 402.

Page 62   "Well, son, I'll tell you": LH, "Mother to Son," *Selected Poems,* 187.

Page 63   "O Blues!": LH, "The Weary Blues," *Selected Poems,* 33.

9. On Top of the Mountain

Quotations from LH, *The Big Sea,* 266, 281.

Page 65   "study and live simply": LH letter to Dean of the College, Lincoln University, Pa., 20 October 1925. Cited in Rampersad, *Life of LH,* 1:116.

"Lincoln is more like": LH to Carl Van Vechten, 26 March 1926. Carl Van Vechten Papers, Yale University.

Page 66   "poet of promise": *New York Times,* as cited in Rampersad, *Life of LH,* 1:129.

Notes

Page 66 "We have tomorrow": LH, excerpt from "Youth," *The Dream Keeper,* 77.

"the mountain standing in the way": LH, "The Negro Artist and the Racial Mountain," *The Nation,* 23 June 1926: 692.

Page 67 "Homesick blues": LH, "Homesick Blues," *Fine Clothes to the Jew,* 24.

"new verse form": Howard Mumford Jones, *Chicago Daily News,* 29 June 1927. Cited in Rampersad, *Life of LH,* 1:145.

"the ones to whom life": LH letter to Dewey Jones of the *Chicago Defender,* 5 February 1927. Cited in Emanuel, *LH,* 31.

Page 70 "I wanted to write": LH, *I Wonder As I Wander,* 5.

Page 71 "like a banner": LH, "Color," *The Panther and the Lash,* 67.

"We build our temples": LH, "The Negro Artist and the Racial Mountain," *The Nation,* 23 June 1926: 694.

10. I, Too, Sing America

Quotations from LH, *I Wonder As I Wander,* 3, 40, 41, 45.

Page 74 "do what I can to encourage": LH to Walter White, 5 August 1931, as cited in Rampersad, *Life of LH* 1: 214. Fisk University Library Special Collections.

Page 75 "Dark ones of Africa": LH, "Sun Song," *Selected Poems,* 5.

"poetry can mean something": LH to Rosenwald Fund (Edwin R. Embree), 17 March 1932, LHP.

Page 76 "original jazz poet": Arna Bontemps, as cited in Meltzer, *LH,* 251.

"I, too, sing America": LH, "I, Too," *Selected Poems,* 275.

11. I Dream a World

Quotations from LH, *I Wonder As I Wander,* 285, 293, 307, 345, 354, 357, 363, 385.

Page 80 "Good morning, Revolution": LH, "Good Morning, Revolution," *New Masses* 7 (September 1932): 5. Reprinted in *Good Morning Revolution,* ed. Berry, 2.

Page 83 "Dear heart": Carrie Clark to LH, LHP.

Page 84 "We Negroes of America": LH, "Too Much of Race," *The Volunteer for Liberty,* (23 August 1937): 3. Reprinted with permission of the Veterans of the Abraham Lincoln Brigade.

"In some lands": LH, "Oppression," *Fields of Wonder,* 112.

Page 86 "I dream a world": LH, "I Dream a World," from *Troubled Island: An Opera,* LHP 3792. Reprinted in Rampersad, *Life of LH,* 2:25. This text is also found in *The LH Reader,* 164 and *American Negro Poetry,* ed. Arna Bontemps (New York: Hill and Wang, 1963, 71-72.)

12. The Dream Keeper

Page 90 "had lots of fun": LH, *I Wonder As I Wander,* 316.

"the boogie-woogie rumble": LH, "Dream Boogie," *Selected Poems,* 221.

Page 90   "laughing to keep from crying": title of LH's book of short stories, 1952.

           "Just me talking to myself": LH, "Simple and Me," *Phylon* 6 (Winter 1945): 349.

Page 91   "drawing from the well": LH, "Bird in Orbit," *Ask Your Mama: Twelve Moods for Jazz,* 91. Reprinted with permission.

           "I am running a literary factory": LH to Arna Bontemps, 21 November 1953, *Arna Bontemps/LH Letters,* ed. Nichols, 317.

           "If you want to die": LH to James Baldwin, 25 July 1953, LHP.

Page 92   "The committee shivers": LH, "Un-American Investigators," *The Panther and the Lash,* 76.

Page 93   "Without them": LH, speech accepting the Spingarn Medal, 26 June 1960, LHP 3304.

           "break through the wall": LH, "As I Grew Older," *Selected Poems,* 11.

Page 94   "Fame is lovely": LH to Arna Bontemps, 23 February 1948, *Arna Bontemps/LH Letters,* ed. Nichols, 229.

           "electric green ink"; "He made me feel": Mari Evans, telephone interview by author, 21 April 1992.

           "married to his work": George Houston Bass, interview by author, 21 October 1989.

           "poet laureate": Lerone Bennett, Jr., *Before the Mayflower: A History of Black America* (Chicago: Johnson Publishing Co., 1961), 560; LH was cited as "the poet laureate of the Negro race" when he was presented with the Spingarn Medal in 1960.

           "He was always smiling": Henri Cartier-Bresson, interview by Rampersad, cited in *Life of LH,* 1:304. Reprinted with permission.

           "I liked that you": Sartur Andrzejewski to LH, 9 May 1926, LHP. Reprinted with permission of Gene J. Andre.

           "used charm as a mask": George Bass, interview.

Page 95   "Bring me all of your dreams": LH, "The Dream Keeper," *The Dream Keeper,* 3.

Hold Fast to Dreams

Page 97   "You will find the whole world": LH, "On Being a Writer," 24 March 1966, LHP 3389.

           "from Africa to Georgia"; "sorrow songs": LH, "The Negro," *Selected Poems,* 8.

           "To fling my arms wide": LH, "Dream Variations," *Selected Poems,* 14.

Page 98   "Hold fast to dreams": LH, "Dreams," *The Dream Keeper,* 7.

Notes

Selected Bibliography

The main source for this book was the writings of Langston Hughes: his poetry, autobiographies, essays, and unpublished letters and papers in the Yale Collection of American Literature, James Weldon Johnson Collection, Beinecke Rare Book and Manuscript Library at Yale University. Arnold Rampersad's two-volume definitive biography, *The Life of Langston Hughes,* was also invaluable for its perspective and as a source for further research.

The following is a partial listing of Hughes's writings, arranged in order of publication. For a more complete bibliography of books he edited and translated, his histories and biographies for children, his song lyrics and dramatic works, see Donald C. Dickinson's *A Bio-Bibliography of Langston Hughes, 1902-1967.*

I. Works by Langston Hughes

Poetry

The Weary Blues. New York: Alfred A. Knopf, 1926.

Fine Clothes to the Jew. New York: Alfred A. Knopf, 1927.

The Dream Keeper and other poems. New York: Alfred A. Knopf, 1932. Revised edition, 1994.

Shakespeare in Harlem. New York: Alfred A. Knopf, 1942.

Fields of Wonder. New York: Alfred A. Knopf, 1947.

One-Way Ticket. New York: Alfred A. Knopf, 1949.

Montage of a Dream Deferred. New York: Henry Holt, 1951.

Selected Poems of Langston Hughes. New York: Alfred A. Knopf, 1959. Reprint, New York: Vintage Books, 1974.

Ask Your Mama: Twelve Moods for Jazz. New York: Alfred A. Knopf, 1961.

The Panther and the Lash: Poems of Our Times. New York: Alfred A. Knopf, 1967. Reprint, New York: Vintage Books, 1992.

The Collected Poems of Langston Hughes. Edited by Arnold Rampersad and David Roessel. New York: Alfred A. Knopf, 1994.

Autobiographies

The Big Sea: An Autobiography. New York: Alfred A. Knopf, 1940. Reprint, New York: Thunder's Mouth Press, 1986.

I Wonder As I Wander: An Autobiographical Journey. New York: Rinehart, 1956. Reprint, New York: Thunder's Mouth Press, 1986.

Fiction

Not Without Laughter. New York: Alfred A. Knopf, 1930.

The Ways of White Folks. New York: Alfred A. Knopf, 1934. Reprint, New York: Vintage Books, 1990.

Laughing to Keep from Crying. New York: Henry Holt, 1952.

Something in Common and Other Stories. New York: Hill and Wang, 1963.

Plays

Don't You Want to Be Free? One Act Play Magazine (October 1938): 359-93.

Five Plays by Langston Hughes. Edited by Webster Smalley. Bloomington, Ind.: Indiana University Press, 1963.

Essays

"The Negro Artist and the Racial Mountain." *The Nation,* 23 June 1926: 692-94.

"Songs Called the Blues." *Phylon* 2 (Summer 1941): 143-45.

"Simple and Me." *Phylon* 6 (Winter 1945): 349-353.

"My Adventures as a Social Poet." *Phylon* 8 (Fall 1947): 205-12.

Humor

The Best of Simple. New York: Hill and Wang, 1961.

Simple's Uncle Sam. New York: Hill and Wang, 1965.

The Return of Simple. Edited by Akiba Harper. New York: Hill and Wang, 1994.

Anthologies

The Langston Hughes Reader. New York: George Braziller, 1958.

Good Morning Revolution: Uncollected Writings of Social Protest by Langston Hughes. Edited by Faith Berry. New York: Lawrence Hill, 1973. Revised edition, New York: Citadel Press, 1992.

II. Letters

Arna Bontemps/Langston Hughes Letters—1925-1967. Edited by Charles H. Nichols. New York: Dodd, Mead and Co., 1980.

III. Interviews

Bass, George Houston. Interview by author. Brown University, Providence, Rhode Island. 21 October 1989.

Evans, Mari. Telephone interview by author, 21 April 1992.

IV. Works about Langston Hughes

Berry, Faith. *Langston Hughes: Before and Beyond Harlem.* Westport, Conn.: Lawrence Hill and Co., 1983. Revised edition, New York: Citadel Press, 1992.

Dickinson, Donald C. *A Bio-Bibliography of Langston Hughes, 1902-1967.* Hamden, Conn.: Shoe String Press, 1967. Revised edition, Hamden, Conn.: Archon Books, 1972.

Emanuel, James A. *Langston Hughes*. New York: Twayne Publishers, 1967.

Huggins, Nathan Irvin. *Harlem Renaissance*. New York: Oxford University Press, 1971.

Jemie, Onwuchekwa. *Langston Hughes: An Introduction to the Poetry*. New York: Columbia University Press, 1976.

Langston Hughes Society. *The Langston Hughes Review*. Athens, Georgia: Institute for African American Studies, University of Georgia. Published two times each year.

Miller, R. Baxter. *The Art and Imagination of Langston Hughes*. Lexington, Kentucky: The University Press of Kentucky, 1989.

O'Daniel, Therman, ed. *Langston Hughes: Black Genius*. New York: William Morrow and Co., 1971.

Rampersad, Arnold. *The Life of Langston Hughes*. 2 vols. New York: Oxford University Press, 1986, 1988.

Scott, Mark. "Langston Hughes of Kansas." *Kansas History: A Journal of the Central Plains* 3 (Spring 1980): 3-25.

Sutton, Paulette D. "Langston in Lawrence." Unpublished essay based on taped interviews for Professor William Tuttle's History 96 at the University of Kansas, 27 April 1972.

Vendler, Helen, ed. *Voices and Visions: The Poet in America*. New York: Random House, 1987. Companion to the PBS television series.

V. Sound and Video Recordings

Grosvener, Verda. *Langston Hughes: The Making of a Poet*. Washington, D.C.: National Public Radio Cassettes, 1988.

Hughes, Langston. *Life Makes Poetry*. Kansas Collection, University of Kansas Libraries. Tape recording of speech, 28 April 1965.

Langston Hughes Reads and Talks about His Poems. St. Petersburg, Florida: Spoken Arts, 1969.

Langston Hughes: The Dream Keeper. In *Voices and Visions*. New York: Center for Visual History, 1988. Videocassette of PBS television series.

VI. Suggestions for Young Readers

Davis, Ossie. *Langston, a Play*. New York: Delacorte Press, 1982.

Hamilton, Virginia. *Many Thousand Gone: African Americans from Slavery to Freedom*. New York: Alfred A. Knopf, 1993.

Harlem Renaissance special issue. Cobblestone 12 (February 1991).

Hughes, Langston. *Don't You Turn Back*. Poems selected by Lee Bennett Hopkins. New York: Alfred A. Knopf, 1969.

_____. *Famous Negro Heroes of America*. New York: Dodd, Mead and Co., 1958.

_____. *The First Book of Jazz.* New York: Franklin Watts, 1955. 3rd edition: *Jazz,* updated and
   expanded by Sandford Brown, 1982.

Katz, William L. and Crawford, Marc. *The Lincoln Brigade, a Picture History.* New York: Atheneum,
   1989.

Meltzer, Milton. *Langston Hughes: A Biography.* New York: Thomas A. Crowell Co., 1968.

Index

Note: Titles are by Langston Hughes unless otherwise noted.

Index